PSYCHOLOGY
IN A WEEK

Nicky Hayes

The Teach Yourself series has been trusted around the world
for over 60 years. This academic series of 'In A Week' books
is designed to help people at all levels and around the world
to discover the basics of key ideas in the fields of philosophy,
religion and culture. Learn in a week, remember for a lifetime.

Dr Nicky Hayes is a fully qualified psychologist who has spent her varied career practising, teaching and communicating psychology. She is the author of a large number of both academic and popular educational titles, including *A Student's Dictionary of Psychology* (with Peter Stratton; 5th edition, 2012) and the Teach Yourself books *Understand Psychology* (2010) and *Understand Applied Psychology* (2010).

PSYCHOLOGY

Nicky Hayes

www.inaweek.co.uk

Teach® Yourself

IN A WEEK

First published in Great Britain in 2011 by Hodder & Stoughton. An Hachette UK company.

First published in US in 2011 by The McGraw-Hill Companies, Inc.

This revised and expanded edition published 2013

Previously published as *Psychology Made Simple*

Copyright © Nicky Hayes 2011, 2013

British Library Cataloguing in Publication Data: a catalogue record for this title is available from the British Library.

Library of Congress Catalog Card Number: on file.

10 9 8 7 6 5 4 3 2

The publisher has used its best endeavours to ensure that any Website addresses referred to in this book are correct and active at the time of going to press. However, the publisher and the author have no responsibility for the Websites and can make no guarantee that a site will remain live or that the content will remain relevant, decent or appropriate.

The publisher has made every effort to mark as such all words which it believes to be trademarks. The publisher should also like to make it clear that the presence of a word in the book, whether marked or unmarked, in no way affects its legal status as a trademark.

Every reasonable effort has been made by the publisher to trace the copyright holders of material in this book. Any errors or omissions should be notified in writing to the publisher, who will endeavour to rectify the situation for any reprints and future editions.

Artworks: Peter Lubach

Typeset by Cenveo® Publisher Services

Printed in and bound Great Britain by CPI Group (UK), CR0 4YY

Hodder & Stoughton policy is to use papers that are natural, renewable and recyclable products and made from wood grown in sustainable forests. The logging and manufacturing processes are expected to conform to the environmental regulations of the country of origin.

Hodder & Stoughton Ltd

338 Euston Road

London NW1 3BH

www.hodder.co.uk

CONTENTS

INTRODUCTION

There are no easy answers to understanding people. Any one person's mind is so complex that we could understand it only by knowing everything about their whole life – and also knowing how their previous learning had led them to interpret and make sense of the experiences that they have had. What we can understand, though, are some of the ways that the mind works, and how different factors combine together. As the science of psychology has developed over the past 150 years or so, psychologists have taken many different approaches to understanding the human mind – often believing that their particular approach would provide all the answers. Nobody has managed that, but each approach has helped to throw light on different parts of the puzzle, and so contribute to the whole picture.

A modern definition of psychology would probably refer to it as the **scientific study of experience and behaviour**. That means that as psychologists we are interested in what people experience as well as what they actually do. More recently, too, psychologists have begun to understand the importance of the **social influences** in our lives – both directly, through the groups, families and communities that we participate in, and indirectly, through our social experience and understanding. We need to put all these types of knowledge together if we really want to understand human beings.

One of the most important lessons that we have learned from the history of psychology is that just looking at one single aspect of experience or behaviour isn't enough. People do things for lots of different reasons, and usually for several reasons at once. If we try to single out just one of those reasons, as if that were the only explanation, then we hit problems straight away. Saying, 'Oh, they're really intelligent' to explain why someone became a research physicist doesn't answer the whole question, because it doesn't tell us why they became interested in science in the first place – or even why they went into an academic career at all, instead of becoming a politician or going into business. Instead, we have to look at what people do from several different angles, to see how all the different factors and influences work together to produce the final outcome.

This is where we come to the idea of **levels of explanation**, or **levels of analysis**. Anything that we do can be studied from several different levels. One psychologist studying reading might use a very general level, such as looking at cultural influences on human behaviour. Another might approach it at the level of social influence, by looking at how family or similar groups affect what we do, and also how we conform to social expectations – or don't, as the case may be. Some psychologists might look at it in terms of personal habits and past experiences, while others would seek to understand how the visual information is processed in the brain. All of these, and many others, are levels of explanation that we can use in our attempt to understand human beings.

AREAS OF PSYCHOLOGY

Psychology, as we've seen, is about people. But people have complex lives, and we need to gather information about them in many different ways. So professional psychologists need to understand the different areas of psychology, and how each of them contributes to our understanding. There are six of these, roughly speaking, and each one gives us a different kind of information:

1 **Cognitive psychology** This includes mental processes such as taking in information and making sense of it (a process we call perception), remembering things, or recognizing them, and also thinking and reasoning.
2 **Social psychology** This is concerned with individual behaviour in a social context – how people influence us, and how we influence them in turn.
3 **Individual psychology** This is concerned with what motivates people, as well as with how people differ from one another.

4 **Physiological psychology**. Sometimes called **bio-psychology**, this is concerned with understanding how our physiological state influences us. Physiological psychologists look at areas such as the effects of brain damage, how drugs work, sleep and dreaming, and understanding stress.

5 **Developmental psychology**. This is concerned with understanding how changes in childhood, adolescence, adulthood and old age affect us, and what those changes actually involve.

6 **Comparative psychology**. This is concerned with animal behaviour in its own right, but also with the study of how animals interact with one another, because this might give us some clues to understanding human beings.

We can see, then, that psychology is really quite a broad topic. It covers a great many levels of explanation, ranging from research at the molecular level as physiological psychologists investigate how drugs work in the brain, to research into the shared beliefs of whole cultures, as social psychologists investigate social representations. And it tries to bring together the insights obtained from these levels, and from the different areas of psychological research, to make sense of what people do and how they understand their worlds.

SUNDAY

Social development and interaction

Today's chapter is about who we are and how we come to be that way. All over the world, babies are brought up in different ways. The experience of an Inuit child, living in a traditional community in the Arctic regions of northern Canada, is widely different from the experience of a child growing up in Papua New Guinea. What we all have in common, though, is that human beings are social animals. The human infant survives because other people take care of it, and teach it what it needs to know.

Human infants are geared towards sociability and adaptability from birth: they communicate with and learn from other people. In childhood and adulthood, too, our self-concept and our understanding of who we are develops through our interactions with others, our wider social experiences and the cultural beliefs that we have acquired from others around us.

THE FIRST RELATIONSHIPS

All over the world, babies are brought up in different ways. In some communities babies are kept tightly wrapped up (swaddled); in others they wear few, if any, clothes. In some communities they are carried around continuously, while in others they spend most of their day in cots or beds. And in some communities they spend all their time with their mothers, while in others they are looked after by relatives, friends, or even older children.

Yet despite all these different conditions, babies grow and, if they survive, generally develop into mature, balanced adults. Human babies can adapt to a tremendous range of different environments and conditions. These differences in how they are looked after don't really matter, as long as a baby gets what it really needs for healthy development. And what it needs most of all is other people.

Human infants are born supremely adapted for sociability. For example, when an infant is first born it is unable to change the focus of its eyes. However, those eyes have a fixed focus at just the right distance to allow the child to look at its mother's face while it is breastfeeding – and this is from the first day after birth.

A human infant inherits a tendency to smile when it sees something which resembles a human face – and as it gets older, the resemblance needs to be more and more exact. For a parent, of course, being looked at and smiled at by your baby is very rewarding and so it means that the parent is more likely to want to spend time with the baby, playing with it and talking to it.

Babies also have a very good way of summoning help when they need it. A baby's cry can carry for a very long distance, and people quickly learn to recognize the sound of their own baby's crying as opposed to that of any other infant.

Infants can communicate more than one message through crying. Back in the 1960s, Wolff recorded baby cries and analysed them using a sound spectrograph, showing that there were at least three different types of cry, with three different patterns of sound: one for pain, one for hunger and one for anger. And the mothers were perfectly able to recognize the message in their own baby's crying. So even an apparently helpless infant is equipped to interact with other people – in other words, to be sociable.

As it grows older, the baby's tendency towards sociability becomes even more apparent. Psychologists have conducted many observations of parent–child interaction and found that most of the things which parents and infants do when they are playing together help the baby to learn skills it will need in childhood and later life.

Babies become especially fond of parents (and other people) who are sensitive to the signals they are giving out – smiling and other facial expressions, movements, and so on – and who are prepared to interact with them in their playing. They don't develop such strong attachments to people who just care for them physically but don't play or talk with them.

THE SELF-CONCEPT

Each of us has our own, personal idea of ourselves – something which is known as the **self-concept**. It's our ideas about what we are like, what we are good or bad at doing, and how we think.

The self-concept is often thought of as having two different parts. One of these is a descriptive part, which is just about what we are like: tall, being good at languages, liking sport, and so on. That part is known as the self-image. The other is an evaluative part, which makes judgements about whether we are good, bad, worthwhile and so on. That part of the self-concept is known as our self-esteem. And that is the part which can be most influential in shaping our relationships with others.

PERSONAL RELATIONSHIPS

Carl Rogers, the famous psychologist who is known as the father of counselling psychology, argued that our level of self-esteem depends on the type of **personal relationships** that we have had. People, Rogers argued, have two basic psychological needs, and will suffer psychological damage if those needs are not met. One of those needs is the need for positive regard from other people – affection, love, trust and so on.

SUNDAY

MONDAY

TUESDAY

WEDNESDAY

THURSDAY

FRIDAY

SATURDAY

Everyone, Rogers argued, needs positive regard of some kind. Even people who avoid close relationships find it important that other people should respect them. To have some kind of positive regard from other people is a very fundamental need, which has to be satisfied.

Positive regard

The other fundamental need which has to be satisfied is the need for **self-actualization**. Self-actualization means making real ('actualizing') the different parts of the self – in other words, exploring and developing our ideas, abilities, interests and talents.

Most people have family, friends and working colleagues who provide them with the positive regard which they need; and hobbies, interests and, if they are lucky, challenging jobs to satisfy their need for self-actualization. And for that reason, Rogers argued, most people have a reasonably high level of self-esteem. While they don't see themselves as being perfect, they are reasonably content with being who they are.

However, Rogers was working as a clinical psychologist and came across a lot of people who weren't in that position.

In these patients, Rogers found that the two needs contradicted one another. Their need for positive regard, or approval from other people, was in direct conflict with their need for self-actualization. These people had come to Rogers because they were suffering from neurotic problems.

When Rogers explored the childhood which these people had experienced, he found that they all had one thing in common. They had all grown up with parents who had made their positive regard conditional on good behaviour. In other words, when they were naughty or had misbehaved – as children often do – they had received a very clear message that they were unloved and unwanted.

So they grew up believing that they had to be ideal and perfect, and that, if they were not, nobody would like them. What this meant was that they needed approval from other people so much that they wouldn't risk exploring their own interests, in case other people didn't like it or didn't approve. They stifled their own personal ambitions, interests or talents – in other words, their need for self-actualization – in order to be sure of social approval.

The solution which Rogers found was very simple. He argued that everyone needs some kind of secure psychological base from which they can develop. That base will be found in a relationship which gives them **unconditional positive regard** – positive regard which doesn't depend on how the person acts.

However, Rogers found that it isn't only parents who can provide this kind of relationship. In fact, we can experience this kind of relationship at any age, and it can provide us with the security that we need to begin to self-actualize. Many people in adult life find relationships which give them that security, and begin to explore aspects of themselves which they have ignored before – like people who go to college for the first time in their 30s or 40s. The important thing is to have a relationship of that kind at all – it doesn't have to be in childhood.

Rogers developed an approach to psychotherapy based on this principle. Many counselling psychologists still use this approach today.

CULTURAL AND SOCIAL INFLUENCES

Our ideas about ourselves and how we are linked with other people are also shaped by the social groups and cultures that we belong to. And different cultures can make very different assumptions about individuals and what it is to be an human being.

In the Western world, it is quite common to see each person as a separate individual, who may choose to link him/herself with some kind of social group if they want to. We tend to believe that it is important to be an individual, in the sense of making one's own decisions about one's life, partners, friends and career. And it is this belief in an individuality which is separate from the other people around us which makes the Western approach rather different from most of the other cultures in the world.

For example, in most of the traditional African cultures, and in Native Australian cultures as well, the person is seen as being primarily a member of the community. That doesn't mean that they are not seen as being an individual person, but it does mean that how they live their life concerns the rest of the community as well, and isn't just their own responsibility. Individualism which doesn't concern itself with the community as a whole is seen as being irresponsible, and pretty well uncivilized.

The idea of the individual as entirely separate from others is really quite an uncommon one. And even in Western cultures, we are not quite as immune to the influence of other people as all that.

SOCIAL IDENTIFICATION

We are all part of society, and each of us belongs to social groups of some kind. Social groups can be large-scale, for example sharing the same gender or ethnic background; they can be medium-scale, like being an accountant or a machinery tuner in a factory; or they can be small-scale, like being a member of a local astronomy club. But whatever their size, belonging to different social groups has an influence on our sense of identity.

We categorize other people as well as other things: this person is a typical Volvo driver, that person is a rock fan, and so on. And we include our own groups – the ones that we belong to – in the classification.

However, there is more to it than that, because it is also a basic human tendency to look for sources of positive self-esteem. If our social group doesn't have much status, then we may try to redefine it or change its perceived social status. But if we can't do that, then we may try to leave the group or, at the very least, pretend that we are not like the other members of it.

It is now much easier for a black child, for example, to grow up being proud of being black than it was 50 years ago. There are far more black people doing responsible, professional jobs, or holding highly respected positions in society than there used to be, which helps. There are also many people in the public eye who are proud of being black, and ready to say so.

This is because over the past 50 years a great many black people have been deliberately changing the perceived status of their group, by challenging stereotypes and discrimination whenever they encounter it. This has had its effect. There is still racism, of course, and still a lot to do, but the general view in Western society is very different from the view which was commonly held – even by black people – 50 years ago.

We can see, then, that who we are and how we see ourselves are very closely linked with the ways in which we interact with other people. We all have our own personal likes, dislikes, talents and personalities. But we also exist in a network of social interaction, and have done so since we were very small babies. Other people's reactions and ideas matter to us, and they influence how we go about acting in life. Our cultural background also shapes how we see ourselves, and so do our social identities. None of us is totally patterned by these social influences – after all, everyone is different – but we are not totally independent of them either.

CO-OPERATION AND COMPLIANCE

In some ways, we have a very good social understanding. But when it comes to modern living, the predictions we make aren't always accurate. For example, people often avoid disagreeing openly with someone else because they imagine that doing so will have more dramatic consequences than it really would. They think the other person might become upset or angry. In fact, we seem to spend a lot of time avoiding other people's imaginary anger, although if we do actually confront someone and disagree with them, it usually isn't nearly as difficult as all that.

Asch (1952) showed just how hard we try to avoid disagreeing openly with other people. He set up a situation in which several people were asked to sit in the same room and to compare various lines with a test line, saying whether they were shorter or longer. The task was very easy, but most of the people in the room were actors who had been told to give obviously wrong answers. Only one unsuspecting person was the real research participant on each occasion. That person could see what the right answer was, but also heard all the other people in the room giving the wrong answer – and the same wrong answer at that! So the participants were forced into a situation where they either had to disagree with the others or lie.

Asch found that about a third of the time the research participants would give the same wrong answer as the others. And even when they gave the right answer, they became extremely nervous and tense just before it was their turn to speak. Later, they said that they had given the correct answer only because they knew it was an experiment and they felt it was their duty to report it accurately. Clearly, disagreeing openly with other people is something they found very difficult.

Co-operating with other people is something which we tend to do almost automatically – at least when those other people are present. When we're away from other people, or after we've had time to think about it, whether we co-operate or not may be quite another matter. But the tendency to avoid disagreement and confrontation is strong, and some studies show that even if other people aren't present, we may still be likely to go along with what we think other people might say.

OBEDIENCE

But what happens when that type of situation could mean that we end up doing something which is morally wrong? We usually obey authority figures, sometimes even if we disagree personally with what they are asking us to do. But would we obey them if they were asking us to, say, give someone a lethal electric shock? The social psychologist Milgram put that question to a sample of psychologists, psychiatrists and other people in the early 1960s. All of them were positive that only a very small minority of people – fewer than 3 per cent – would be prepared to kill or seriously harm another person in obedience to the demands of a psychological experiment.

The human tendency to obey...

So Milgram decided to set up a situation in which people would believe their actions were being seriously harmful, even though nobody would actually be hurt. He advertised for volunteers and, when they arrived, they were told that it was an experiment about punishment and learning. The volunteers were to act as 'experimenters', who would give increasing electric shocks to a 'subject' in the next room by pressing switches each time the 'subject' got an answer wrong.

The switches were clearly labelled as being of increasing severity, and went up to 450 volts; and the 'subject' (who was really an actor) said at the beginning of the study that he had a weak heart. Both the labels on the switches and the sounds which came from the other room implied that the person was in serious pain as the voltage increased, before the victim fell ominously silent. Even then, the 'experimenter' was told to keep giving the shocks by a grey-coated supervisor who oversaw the whole operation and insisted that they should continue.

There were a lot of things about the situation which encouraged obedience, such as the way that each electric shock was only a little bit stronger than the one before. That made it very hard for someone to draw a line and say, 'I won't go any further', because what they were being asked to do next wasn't very different from what they had already done. Some people stopped anyway when they felt they had gone far enough. They knew, in their own minds, that to go further would be wrong and that was enough. They didn't feel any need to justify or rationalize what they were doing.

REBELLION

Milgram showed us how easy unthinking obedience is for many people. But a third of the people in his study refused to obey once things reached the point where they felt that the 'subject' was in danger. When they were interviewed afterwards, these people generally turned out to have had some previous experience with unthinking obedience and what it could do – for example, having experienced it in Nazi Germany.

Milgram found that nearly two-thirds of the people he tested would carry on obeying the supervisor even to the very highest shock level. That didn't mean that they liked doing it: they would argue and point out that the 'subject' needed help, and try to refuse to do any more. They became very distressed indeed. But the supervisor would insist that they continue, and in the end they would obey.

So it's apparent that we will refuse to obey other people if we are clear enough about what is going on and how we are being manipulated. Sometimes it's important to disagree. All the great social reforms which took place in the eighteenth century, for instance, began as the dedicated campaigns of a handful of people who saw something wrong and did not let it rest. Slavery was widely accepted in Europe in the eighteenth century but, as a result of consistent campaigning, the slave trade was made illegal in the early years of the nineteenth century, and the owning of slaves became illegal some years later. Moscovici and Nemeth (1974) showed that, if just a few people stick to a particular view, which they are convinced is right, then over time they can have a great deal of influence on a larger group. The important thing, though, is that those people who are in the minority and trying to influence the majority should be seen to be genuine and consistently resisting social pressure.

UNDERSTANDING OTHER PEOPLE

We actually spend quite a lot of time thinking about what other people think. From a very young age, we develop what is known as a **theory of mind** – an awareness of other people as thinking, feeling individuals – which we use to interact effectively with other people.

Psychologists have found that most children develop a theory of mind sometime between the ages of three and four. The child becomes aware that other people think and see the world differently and that its own experience isn't necessarily shared by everyone else.

Deliberate communication depends on being able to guess what the other person will think, so that we can make our messages clear. If we don't know that the other person is thinking independently, we can't engage in the give-and-take which conversation needs.

Communication isn't always deliberate, though. We pass information to one another in all sorts of ways, and sometimes we may not even realize that we have done it. This type of communication is known as **non-verbal communication** – communication without words.

As a general rule, we use non-verbal communication automatically, without thinking about it. Facial expressions, body language, gestures and tones of voice are all important indicators of our feelings and attitudes. In any interpersonal situation it is important for us to pick up on feelings and attitudes, if only so that we can get some idea of how we should be responding to them.

Non-verbal communication has been studied extensively by psychologists because there are so many different ways in which we communicate messages to one another, and so many messages contained within any episode of human interaction.

One of the most interesting findings has been that people tend to believe non-verbal communication far more than they believe the words that we actually say.

VERBAL COMMUNICATION AND DISCOURSE

People also convey quite a lot of extra information in the actual words that they choose, as well as the way in which they say them. Looking at how people express themselves has become a major source of interest in modern psychology. It's known as **discourse analysis**, because the researchers who are doing it are analysing the patterns of discourse or conversation.

For example, when people are discussing complex topics like politics or the state of society, they often try out different images, and then, as the conversation progresses, settle on a single metaphor. Using the same type of image helps the people in the conversation to frame the problems that they are discussing and identify possible solutions. Another part of discourse analysis involves looking directly at the explanations which people give for why things happen.

The process of ascribing reasons for why things happened and why people acted in certain ways is known as **attribution**. One of the interesting things about how we use attributions is that we almost always judge other people's actions differently from the way we judge our own. We make situational attributions for ourselves – seeing our actions as a result of the situation we are in. But when we are judging someone else's actions, we generally use dispositional attributions – we conclude that the reason why they are doing something is because of their personality or character. It's known as the **fundamental attribution error**, and we do it even when we know that the situation is really the most important influence.

SOCIAL REPRESENTATIONS

A lot of our thinking is shaped by the shared explanations held by our own social groups, or by society in general. These shared explanations are known as **social representations** and they can be a very powerful influence in society.

Wagner and Hayes (2005) showed how we draw from social influences and factors to make sense of our lives – to tell ourselves the 'stories' which shape and direct our actions. Those stories are closely influenced by the social groups we belong to and the cultures that we come from, and understanding them is important in understanding why human beings – and societies – behave as they do.

How we explain things to ourselves also has quite an influence on how we interact with other people. For example, if we come across someone who is asking for help, whether we actually step in and help them or not depends on how we define the situation – and that in turn will depend on the social representations we are using. If we conclude that the situation isn't really serious, or that it is the person's own fault that they are in that situation, then we are much less likely to help out than if we define it differently.

Then there are the **social scripts** which are present in most situations. If we go to a restaurant, for instance, there is a definite script which tells us when we should do certain things and when we can expect things to happen. We'd be deeply disconcerted if the waiter brought coffee before the main course, for instance, and we would wonder what was going on.

Social scripts are closely linked with social representations, but they operate at a more specific level. Where social representations tell us the overall 'story' of why things are happening, social scripts tell us what behaviour seems to be appropriate in a given situation. It is for this reason that so many psychologists are concerned about the large amount of negative drama on TV and in film. It isn't about people copying behaviour directly, although that can happen occasionally. It is more because these dramas provide people with social scripts which suggest that this is an appropriate or normal way to behave. In doing so, they place an unrealistic emphasis on the less pleasant options for human interaction, and encourage people to think it is normal to deal with other people aggressively or vindictively.

SUMMARY

Today we have looked at our social identity and self-concept and how these are largely shaped by our interactions with others – from the members of our family, through our peers, to the social group to which we belong and, at the broadest level, to our society as a whole. In Western and globalized societies there is a tendency to see the individual almost as an 'island', but most psychologists would argue that human flourishing takes place where not only the individual but the group to which he or she belongs is held in positive regard.

Social interactions, as we have also learned today, have a darker aspect too, as witnessed by people's willingness to conform and to comply with rules and orders, even when they know these to be wrong. Often such compliance is motivated by a desire to win approval and to boost our self-esteem. Late twentieth-century research into this tendency has drawn on the lessons learned from totalitarian regimes under which people committed or excused the most terrible atrocities, simply because they were 'obeying orders'.

SUNDAY

MONDAY

TUESDAY

WEDNESDAY

THURSDAY

FRIDAY

SATURDAY

FACT-CHECK (ANSWERS AT THE BACK)

1. Babies are born with a tendency toward...
a) Mistrust ❑
b) Aggression ❑
c) Sociability ❑
d) Individuality ❑

2. What makes up an individual's self-concept?
a) Self-image plus self-esteem ❑
b) The opinion of others ❑
c) Self-esteem plus societal approval ❑
d) None of the above ❑

3. Which *two* of the following, according to Carl Rogers, promote self-esteem?
a) A happy childhood ❑
b) Positive regard ❑
c) Self-actualization ❑
d) Family life ❑

4. Unconditional positive regard can be found...
a) Only during childhood ❑
b) Only during adulthood ❑
c) Only within the family ❑
d) At any age ❑

5. Traditional societies emphasize the importance of...
a) The individual ❑
b) The family ❑
c) The community ❑
d) None of the above ❑

6. How might you best define someone's social identity?
a) Their sense of being part of social groups ❑
b) Their ability to project their personality in a social setting ❑
c) The way they dress and behave ❑
d) None of the above ❑

7. Asch argued that people have a tendency to...
a) Disagree with one other ❑
b) Argue with one other ❑
c) Lie to one another ❑
d) Avoid open disagreement ❑

8. What did Milgram's research show? That the majority of people...
a) Will refuse to do something they think is wrong ❑
b) Will comply with orders ❑
c) Will willingly harm others ❑
d) Will always say 'no' if they disagree ❑

9. What, in psychology, is the theory of mind?
a) The idea that people have an existence independent of their body ❑
b) An awareness that we can never know anybody else ❑
c) An awareness that other people have independent minds ❑
d) None of the above ❑

10. In judging other people's actions, we tend to...

a) Try to imagine ourselves in their shoes ❑

b) Attribute them to their personality ❑

c) Excuse them in the hope they will excuse ours ❑

d) Attribute them to their situation ❑

MONDAY

Emotions and states of mind

Today we will look at emotions and how these can be influenced by our broader state of mind. When we think about emotions, we tend to think only about the negative ones – fear, anger and distress. But this is because the mass media over-emphasizes negative emotions and underplays positive ones, so we often neglect or fail to recognize the positive aspects of everyday life. Our positive emotions are as varied and subtle as our negative ones.

We also have a tendency to downplay the role played by our biological rhythms. We are more dominated by our biological rhythms than we realize. All human beings have circadian rhythms, which produce changes in our ability to perform certain tasks at different times of day. Disruption to these rhythms produces jet lag, which can affect shift workers as well as people who travel to different time zones.

We have many different states of consciousness. Sometimes we feel wide awake and alert; sometimes we feel pensive and dreamy; sometimes we feel drowsy and tired. Psychologists have also shown that the time we spend dreaming is important for organizing and processing the mass of information with which we have been bombarded during our waking hours.

SUNDAY

MONDAY

TUESDAY

WEDNESDAY

THURSDAY

FRIDAY

SATURDAY

POSITIVE EMOTIONS

When we think of emotions, it is generally the unpleasant ones which come to mind: fear, anger, anxiety and so on. This is partly because we live in a society which tends to emphasize those much more than the positive ones. So we tend not to notice the positive emotions that we feel, or to dismiss them as not really important. There are roughly eight kinds of positive emotion. These are listed in Table 1.

Table1 Types of positive emotion

Positive emotion	Description
Potency	Feeling capable and able to do whatever is needed
Spirituality	Feelings of wonder or awe, such as when listening to a particularly beautiful piece of music, or enjoying nature
Contentment	Feeling pleasantly satisfied with circumstances
Relaxation	Feeling unstressed and mentally calm
Self-indulgence	E.g. pampering yourself. Not selfish, but a pleasure which is personal rather than shared
Altruism	Sharing or caring for other people
Absorption	Feeling interested in a topic or a hobby
Exhilaration	Being excited about something, or thrilled by an unexpected pleasant experience

LOVING

We hear about love all the time, through the mass of romantic images in the media. But how far does the public image of 'love' actually reflect the reality? What is really involved in the experience of love, and what is the difference in the love between a couple who have been married for 30 years and that between two starry-eyed teenagers? Are there different kinds of loving?

One of the most useful distinctions was made by Tennov (1979), who argued that love, as a long-term emotion, is actually very different from the short-term, intensive infatuation which we also call love, or being 'in love'. She suggested that it would be more appropriate if we used the

A rush of exhilaration...

term **limerence** to describe the intensive experiences, and kept the term love to refer to longer-term affections and partnerships.

Limerence, according to Tennov (and a vast number of writers, playwrights and musicians), is an intense, all-consuming passion, which has a very strong element of fantasy in it. The person becomes totally obsessed with their idea of their loved one and spends a great deal of time thinking about them and daydreaming. Often, these thoughts are focused around tokens of some kind, such as a letter, a lock of hair or a photograph.

Dimensions of love

Sternberg (1988) went on to look at what is involved in the longer-term emotion which we also call 'love'. He concluded that love seems to consist of three underlying dimensions, with different proportions of these dimensions producing different kinds of love. These dimensions are intimacy, passion and commitment.

Different combinations of these dimensions produce different kinds of love. For example, the kind of long-term companionate love which develops between two people who have been together for many years is often one which is high in intimacy and commitment, but perhaps less so on the passion dimension. Romantic love, on the other hand, tends to be high on intimacy and passion, but doesn't involve as much commitment. Sternberg referred to the kind of love which involves all three dimensions fully as consummate love.

NEGATIVE EMOTIONS

Both anger and fear are very active emotions. If you are angry with someone, your muscles tense up and you become restless: some people will even stand up and pace around the room as a way of helping to control the tension. Similarly, if you are frightened your muscles become tense and you may make small involuntary movements which express that tension.

In the natural world, if an animal is threatened by something so that it becomes frightened, then there are only two options. It can stay and fight, in which case it will need all the strength it can muster, to win; or it can run away, in which case it will need all the strength it can muster, to escape. In either case, therefore, the animal will need all its strength because holding anything back isn't much use if you end up dead. So the animal's body goes into overdrive, to give it as much energy as possible; this is known as the **'fight-or-flight' response**. Humans have it too.

Most of the time, we use only a small proportion of our potential strength and energy. However, during the fight-or-flight response, the body changes the way in which it operates physically in several different ways, all of which help to release more energy to the muscles.

The fight-or-flight response is a very powerful reaction, which serves an important survival function – at least, when we are faced with threats that require physical action. It isn't quite as helpful when we are faced with non-physical threats, such as anxiety about the mortgage, or a fear of failing exams. Because these threats don't require physical action, we don't have a way of using up that energy, and can quickly become stressed.

There are lesser degrees of the fight-or-flight response, too. When our attention is caught by something, or when we feel anxious about something, we experience the same kinds of physical changes but to a much lesser degree. The changes are strong enough to be measured, though, using sensitive detectors that will identify changes in pulse rate, heart rate, sweating, blood pressure and the like. A machine which measures several of these changes is known as a polygraph. Some people use polygraphs as lie detectors because they can detect the slight anxiety which people feel when they tell a lie.

STRESS AND COPING

If we have a fright, or if we become angry with someone, the emotion often passes. We calm down and get over it and, as we do, the physical symptoms of arousal disappear as well. But sometimes we can experience emotional arousal which doesn't go away. Being anxious about whether there will be enough money to pay the bills, for instance, is a continuous worry, not a passing thing. This means that it is constantly producing physiological arousal, which doesn't go away.

Selye (1956) showed that long-term arousal such as this can have many harmful effects, including interfering with our physical health. We call it **stress**, and it is a big problem in modern society. Long-term stress suppresses the action of the body's immune system, making us much more vulnerable to colds, infections and more serious illnesses. It may also make us more liable to contract heart disease. Long-term stress also makes us very jumpy and alert to potential threats – which means that quite often we see something as a threat when it is really quite harmless. Because we overreact to what people say or do, we become more likely to quarrel with the people around us. And it interferes with judgement, so that we are less likely to make sensible decisions or to appraise what is going on realistically.

There are ways of coping with long-term stress so that we do not suffer these effects. Some of these strategies are physical ones which involve using the adrenaline constructively, to give additional energy when exercising. People who do a lot of sport often do better in exams than people of the same intellectual level who don't take regular exercise, and one possible reason for this is that they simply don't experience as much physical stress.

Many coping strategies, though, are cognitive – they involve the person's thinking in some way. They include mental exercises and ways of using the imagination positively. By doing this, we can make sure that the thoughts we have are useful, and won't simply add to the amount of stress we feel.

LOCUS OF CONTROL

People who see themselves as able to control events by hard work and effort, and who don't give up, are much less likely to become depressed, and much more likely to be able actually to do something about their situation, because they keep looking for ways to change it. These people have what is known as an internal **locus of control**. They believe that what happens to them is largely controlled by their own efforts.

Having an internal locus of control is much healthier for a human being – both physically and mentally. Long-term stress can lower the body's resistance to disease and make us vulnerable to illness. But people with an internal locus of control experience less stress, even though their physical situation may be just as bad. This is because they channel their energies into looking for positive things to do, instead of just worrying. And because they are likely to gain at least a small success through trying so hard, they experience positive emotions like a sense of achievement, which people who are more passive don't feel.

Cognitive therapy is all about teaching people how to take control of their own lives, and how to avoid the self-defeating beliefs and attributions which have stopped them from doing so in the past. Almost anything which increases someone's self-confidence has the effect of giving them more of an internal locus of control over their own life. Problems may be real, and not likely to go away, but we can make their effects worse or better, depending on how we go about dealing with them.

POSITIVE PSYCHOLOGY

Positive psychology is about helping people to obtain a more balanced perspective, by learning to recognize and value the positive aspects of our everyday life. Effectively, as its founder Martin Seligman (1998) says, it is about **happiness**. As we have seen, being happier can help us in many ways – even physically, as researchers have shown how positive and happy thoughts can stimulate the immune system and help us to recover from many of our ailments and illnesses. A better awareness of positive psychology could help us all to live life more easily.

We all have the capacity to live a positive life, but we don't all do it in the same way. Martin Seligman (2003) identified three sorts of desirable life: the pleasant life, the good life, and the meaningful life. Effectively, a pleasant life is one in which the person is aware of, and enjoys, positive emotions about the past, present and future. A good life, in Seligman's terms, involves using your strengths and virtues to obtain gratification in the main areas of your life. Finally, a meaningful life is the use of your strengths and virtues in the service of something much larger than you are.

If we generally hold on to an optimistic outlook, and adopt positive coping strategies to deal with our stresses, we can all learn to be happier and healthier as a result.

The importance of positive thinking has been known for a long time. One method used by therapists is called the Pollyanna technique, after a children's book written in the early twentieth century. It involves looking for something good – no matter how small – to come out of every event or disaster. That doesn't mean we have to ignore or belittle the problems, of-course, but it means that we need to see things more realistically. Even apparently awful events can sometimes have positive side effects. Seligman showed how optimism is a much more positive state of mind, and that we can learn to become more optimistic with the right therapy or self-training. Essentially, he showed people how to replace learned helplessness with learned optimism, and have a more positive life as a result.

BIOLOGICAL RHYTHMS

Our state of consciousness changes all the time. We may be in a good mood and then something happens which puts us in a bad one. We may feel sleepy, but then an alarming experience brings us fully alert. We may be relaxed, but the sight of someone we really want to talk to can rouse us to an unexpected level of energy. All of these are changes in consciousness. Sometimes, we change our state of consciousness deliberately by using a drug, such as alcohol or caffeine. But a lot of the time our state of consciousness changes simply because of biological rhythms.

Many people experience a form of depression during the long winter months, which clears up completely when spring and summer come. **Seasonal affective disorder (SAD)**, as this kind of depression is called, has a great deal to do with a lack of natural daylight. After all, for many people who work indoors, in factories or offices, it is possible to pass several months in the winter only seeing natural daylight at weekends. It is dark when we go out to work or college, and dark again when we return home.

Special lamps which mimic daylight have been very successful in treating seasonal affective disorder. The person spends a period of each day exposing their face to the light produced by these lamps, and that stimulates hormones and neurotransmitters in the body and brain which help to reduce the depression.

We have other rhythms which are connected with the 24-hour cycle of the day. These are known as **circadian rhythms**, and they actually influence a great deal of our day-to-day experience. Through the course of the 24-hour cycle, we experience a regular increase and decrease of activity in several physiological systems, including body temperature, blood pressure, pulse rate, blood sugar level and hormone levels. Our moods, alertness, concentration, skills and abilities also vary according to this cycle.

For example, between the hours of two and six in the morning, our blood sugar levels are low, body temperature is low, and so is blood pressure. If we are awake, we generally experience quite a subdued mood; and if we are trying to do a demanding task of some kind, we are much more likely to make mistakes. But this isn't just from tiredness, because as soon as morning comes, we begin to feel better, and more alert, and our performance improves. On the other hand, the hours between eleven and about three o'clock have been shown to be our best times for classroom learning. Before and after those hours, school pupils work best with individualized tasks.

There are other changes which occur during the course of the day. For example, psychologists have shown that the time between about four and six in the evening is by far the best time for exercise – the body gains more benefit from exercise at that time than from the same amount of exercise at other times of the day. Many people experience a slight 'dip' around about 6 p.m., and then find that their energy levels gradually rise for the rest of the evening, until they drop again when it is time to go to bed. Figure 1 shows the highs and lows of body temperature rhythms during a 24-hour period. Psychological alertness often follows a similar cycle.

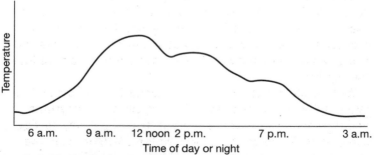

Figure 1 Body temperature throughout the 24-hour cycle

SUNDAY
MONDAY
TUESDAY
WEDNESDAY
THURSDAY
FRIDAY
SATURDAY

SHIFT WORK AND JET LAG

Sometimes our body rhythms are disrupted, so that we have to be alert at different times of the day or night. There are two common reasons for this: shift work and international travel. When we are doing shift work, we have to adjust our bodies to a different 24-hour rhythm, sleeping at different times of the day and being awake at times when we would normally be asleep. When we are travelling across time zones, we also have to adjust to a different rhythm of activity.

Both cases produce the same type of problem, which we call **jet lag** when it is brought about by travel. Although people can adapt to working at odd times, in that they are not aware of being particularly stressed, human performance is always influenced by circadian rhythms. Nobody works as efficiently as they would do at their optimal times of day and, at its worst, it can produce irritability, poor performance at work and poor decision-making.

There are some ways in which the damaging effects of shift work can be minimized. For example, it seems to be easier for people to move forwards in time, rather than backwards. So a shift-work cycle which progresses through the 24-hour period, with someone going from a night shift to an early one, then from an early shift to a late one, and then on to nights again, is much easier for people to adjust to than a shift cycle in which someone goes from an afternoon shift to an early morning one. It's a simple thing, but it can lead to a measurable decrease in industrial accidents or errors at work.

In international travel, too, shifting the 24-hour system forwards (for example, by staying awake for a longer period than you might do normally) can be helpful in minimizing jet lag, and help the person become adapted. Without that, it can take anything up to ten days to get fully adapted to the new cycles. As a result, some politicians or business people who need to make flying visits to countries on the other side of the world decide to cope by sticking rigidly to their 'home' timetables for meals and sleeping, and fitting meetings in between; rather than trying to make the transition to new times and then having to re-adjust a day or so later.

STUDYING THE BRAIN

Brain cells – in fact all nerve cells – work by generating tiny amounts of electricity and passing these on to one another. Some psychologists study brain activity, and how the brain works, by studying the electrical activity of the brain. One way of doing this is by using **electro-encephalographs**, or EEGs for short. These are charts of the brain's electrical activity, which has been detected using small electrodes that are attached to the scalp. The changes are recorded by a pen which rests on a moving sheet of paper and makes small movements whenever the electrical activity varies.

Of course, all of this is a bit like standing outside a factory and trying to guess what they are making by listening to the noises coming through the window. Studying the brain in this way doesn't tell us everything, by any means. But it can show us something about the overall patterns of activity, and one of the things it can show us is the general patterning of brain activity when we are in different states of consciousness. The type of EEG which is produced when we are awake and concentrating on something is very different from the pattern produced when we are awake but just lazily relaxed.

SCANNING THE BRAIN

Recently, we have become able to get a better picture of how the brain works by using scanning techniques. One type of scan, known as a **PET scan** (short for positron emission tomography), involves looking at how much blood is being used by a particular part of the brain. Each time a nerve cell fires, it uses up some nutrients, and so it needs to replace them from the blood supply. So parts of the brain which are being active need a larger blood supply than those which aren't. The PET scan allows a psychologist or doctor to see which parts of the brain are using most blood. It works by 'labelling' the blood using a special radioactive chemical which can be detected by the scanner.

Another type of brain scan is known as computed axial tomography, or **CAT scan**. This involves building up a three-dimensional X-ray picture of the brain, by using X-rays to photograph a set of 'slices' through it. The different images from the 'slices' are then combined using a computer. This can highlight areas of deformed or damaged tissue, such as blood clots or regions where the blood supply has been interrupted. CAT scans can help us to identify exactly where a problem is located.

A third technique is magnetic resonance imaging, or **MRI scanning**. This involves passing a succession of electromagnetic waves – like radio waves – through the brain. The neurones of the brain respond to the electromagnetic stimulation by producing electromagnetic waves themselves, which are detected and recorded. As with CAT scanning, it is the computerized combination of these measurements which produces an image of the brain, this time showing the bundles of nerve fibres.

Scanning techniques have helped us to learn a great deal more about the functioning of 'normal' brains, but we are still a long way from getting a comprehensive understanding of what is going on. Nonetheless, researchers are slowly building up a picture of some of the principles of how the brain works, and which parts do what.

Dreaming plays an important role in sorting out our waking experience

DREAMING

In the early days of psychology, the psychoanalysts, led by Sigmund Freud, believed that dreams come from the unconscious mind, telling us about our innermost secret wishes and desires. These are disguised by the brain, using symbols to stand for the real meaning. The books about dream interpretation that you sometimes see on railway and airport bookstalls are following this idea, but most psychologists do not believe that dream symbolism is quite as important as Freud maintained, even though they may accept that it has some part to play.

Dreaming plays an important part in how we organize our psychological experience. Throughout each day, we are bombarded with a massive amount of sensory information and experiences. At some time, the mind needs to make sense of it all: to store information in its proper place so that it connects with similar things that we know; to identify patterns in our experiences; and to filter through things that have happened to us to identify particularly meaningful events. It does this while we are dreaming.

This explains, too, why sleeping on a problem is so often helpful. Before we go to bed, we may be perplexed, upset or completely at a loss as to how to deal with something. But when we wake up, it often all seems clear. This is because we have been working on the problem unconsciously while we sleep. The brain activity which takes place while we dream has allowed us to knit loose ends together, and to put things, mentally, into their proper place. So when we wake up it is much easier to decide what to do.

We have seen, then, how consciousness is not always constant. It can be changed, influenced or affected in different ways, and it varies of itself during the course of the day or while we are sleeping. Understanding how our human state of consciousness is constantly changing and what sort of experiences affect it can help us to use our awareness to help ourselves – for example, by arranging our days so that we are doing the most intensive work when we are best suited for it; or by using legal drugs such as caffeine or alcohol in ways that will help to optimize our lives rather than damage them.

SUMMARY

Today we have looked at our emotions and how our state of mind can play a role in producing them. Whereas emotions are usually short-lived and intense, state of mind refers to moods, which are often less specific and less intense. Emotions, we have seen, can be either positive or negative, but culturally we often tend to overemphasize negative emotions at the expense of positive ones. This is a pity because, by focusing on our positive emotions, we can draw great benefit from the everyday happinesses and pleasures that are near at hand. Cognitive therapy aims at teaching us to minimize and control the effects of negative emotions.

Controlling our state of mind is perhaps a more difficult task, because we are all subject to physiological changes in our bodies that can make us more vulnerable to negative emotion. Learning to appreciate the body's natural rhythms can improve our mood. Getting enough sleep is vital, too, so that, through dreaming, we can sort out and file away our experiences of the previous day.

SUNDAY

MONDAY

TUESDAY

WEDNESDAY

THURSDAY

FRIDAY

SATURDAY

FACT-CHECK (ANSWERS AT THE BACK)

1. Which of the following is *not* a negative emotion?
   a) Envy ❑
   b) Anger ❑
   c) Absorption ❑
   d) Fear ❑

2. Why do we tend to overemphasize negative emotions?
   a) Because they are more common ❑
   b) Because they are more exciting ❑
   c) Because mass culture focuses on them ❑
   d) None of the above ❑

3. What, according to Tennov, is limerance?
   a) Infatuation ❑
   b) Commitment ❑
   c) Feeling edgy ❑
   d) Intimacy ❑

4. Which of the following is *not* one of the dimensions of love as outlined by Sternberg?
   a) Passion ❑
   b) Commitment ❑
   c) Trust ❑
   d) Intimacy ❑

5. How might a psychologist define stress?
   a) Another word for pressure ❑
   b) Having too much to do and not enough time to do it in ❑
   c) Long-term, potentially harmful arousal ❑
   d) None of the above ❑

6. What, according to Seligman, is a 'good life'?
   a) A life spent doing good deeds ❑
   b) A life spent gaining gratification from one's strengths and virtues ❑
   c) A life spent growing vegetables ❑
   d) A life spent having fun ❑

7. What is seasonal affective disorder?
   a) A disorder bought on by too much summer heat ❑
   b) Depression produced by lack of sunlight in winter ❑
   c) An intense dislike of Christmas or other winter festivals ❑
   d) None of the above ❑

8. What is the name given to our day-to-day rhythms?
   a) Arcadian ❑
   b) Biocycles ❑
   c) Nocturnal ❑
   d) Circadian ❑

9. What is a CAT scan?
   a) A way to measure the electrical activity in the brain ❑
   b) A three-dimensional x-ray image of the brain ❑
   c) A way to measure blood usage by different parts of the brain ❑
   d) A way of seeing the dreams that someone is having ❑

10. What is a PET scan?

a) A way to measure the electrical
activity in the brain ❏

b) A three-dimensional x-ray
image of the brain ❏

c) A way to measure blood
usage by different parts
of the brain ❏

d) A way of seeing the dreams
that someone is having ❏

SUNDAY

MONDAY

TUESDAY

WEDNESDAY

THURSDAY

FRIDAY

SATURDAY

TUESDAY

Motivation

Why do we do what we do? Human motivation is multi-level and complex. We have physiological needs, like hunger or thirst, and established behaviours, like habits, which are hard to break. Our beliefs, personal constructs and social representations can shape how we receive information, so that two people may experience the same events completely differently. And our perceptions can also be affected by unconscious defence mechanisms, where the mind tries to defend itself against perceived threats.

High self-efficacy beliefs help us to have a sense of personal agency, and can lead directly to positive achievement, while learned helplessness reduces it. And one of the most important human motivators of all – our need for social acceptance and respect – can make all the difference to our actions. Our psychological needs can be organized into a hierarchy, but what people do is really much more complex than simple models suggest.

PHYSICAL AND BEHAVIOURAL MOTIVES

Sometimes what we do is motivated by very basic needs: if you go to the kitchen and fetch a glass of water, it's a fair bet that you do it because you are thirsty. The level of fluid in your body has dropped below its ideal level, and this sets off a complex range of physiological mechanisms in the body. Messages about your fluid level are passed from your body to a particular part of the brain, known as the hypothalamus. This sends messages to the cerebral cortex, which is the part of the brain that you think with, so you realize that you feel thirsty and go to get a drink of water.

These mechanisms are all concerned with getting the right balance in the body. As long as everything is at the right kind of level, we don't feel the motivation. But if something becomes imbalanced, for instance if our blood sugar level gets too low or if we don't have a high enough level of fluid in the body, then we take action to put it right. This is known as maintaining **homeostasis** – maintaining the appropriate balance in the body so that we can function well, physically.

Sometimes what we do comes about as much because of habit as anything else. **Habits** are behaviours or feelings that are associated with particular settings or situations. We learn how to act in certain places, or with certain people, and these habits of behaviour come back to us if we find ourselves in that situation again. At such times, we can surprise ourselves with how we react.

Habits can be broken, though – we're not stuck with them for ever. Breaking a habit involves replacing the actions or feelings triggered by that situation with some other actions or feelings. It is hard at first, but the more often you succeed, the weaker the original habit becomes.

COGNITIVE MOTIVES

Cognitive motives are motives which come from our thoughts, beliefs and ideas. They are to do with how we understand what is happening to us, which can make all the difference to what we decide to do about it.

Each of us has had our own personal experiences, and we have learned from them. In particular, we have formed our own personal theories about what other people are like from how people have interacted with us in the past. These theories are called **personal constructs** and we use them when we meet new people.

Since each of us has led a different life, our personal constructs are unique. They represent our own distinctive way of looking at the world. Two people could meet a third person for the first time, and even though they had the same objective experience, they might come to very different conclusions. One, for example, might see the new person as being friendly and outgoing, whereas the other might see them as ingratiating and manipulative. Just because we are in the same situation doesn't mean that we see things the same way.

There are other ways that our minds can motivate us. Many psychologists are deeply sceptical about the ideas of Sigmund Freud, the psychoanalyst who developed a theory about the unconscious mind at the end of the nineteenth century. But Freud did identify some important mental processes which the mind uses to protect itself against threats. These are called **defence mechanisms** and they include the idea of denial (refusing to admit the reality of painful events or situations), the idea that sometimes forgetting may happen because of unconscious motives, and the observation that buried conflicts may cause irrational outbursts of anger. Even modern psychologists, who don't generally share Freud's views about the workings of the unconscious mind, have found the idea of defence mechanisms useful.

Another way that our cognitions can motivate us to action is to do with our **self-efficacy beliefs**. These are our beliefs about how effective we are at doing things – how capable, or how skilled, we are. They are very important, because they affect how hard we try. Bandura (1989) showed how it is generally a good thing if people have high self-efficacy beliefs because it makes them more self-confident and more likely to succeed. It's even a good thing to believe that you are better at things than you actually are – because that way, you will take on more challenges and improve your abilities as you deal with them!

It's not hard to see why having high self-efficacy beliefs helps you to do well. Obviously, if you are prepared to put effort into learning, so you keep trying and learning from your mistakes, then you will eventually get somewhere – even if you are working at something that doesn't come easily to you. Many psychologists nowadays believe that bringing up children and training adults to believe in their own ability to take effective action is one of the most important things of all.

There's another side to this, as well. Some people go through a series of demoralizing or unpleasant experiences, which they can't do anything about, and then they just give up trying altogether. So when they are in a situation which they could actually change if they made an effort, they don't bother. This is known as **learned helplessness** – they have learned to be passive and helpless, rather than trying to influence what happens to them.

It is important for us to feel that we have some control over what happens to us. To feel that you are helpless is very stressful, which just makes things worse. So one way that psychologists try to help these people is to set up situations which will help them to raise their self-efficacy beliefs. By doing something competently, the person comes to realize that they can be effective – that they can actually do something about their situation.

SOCIAL MOTIVATION

What we do is motivated by social influences as well as cognitive ones. One of the most important social motives of all is for respect from other people. We all feel a deep need to avoid looking foolish, and sometimes, if we feel that we have made ourselves look stupid in front of the wrong people, even the memory of it can continue to embarrass us for a long time.

Harré (1979) identified the need for **social respect** as a very basic social motive. A great deal of what we do, Harré argued, is aimed to ensure that people take us seriously, or at least

The desire for social respect...

notice us, and acknowledge us as worthwhile people. We hate it if other people just dismiss us or, worse still, ignore our existence.

SOCIAL REPRESENTATIONS

It is noticeable that violent racist incidents increase when the economy is in recession. Recent events in Europe are an example of this, as was the massive increase of racism in Germany and elsewhere during the 1930s depression – an increase which made the concentration camps possible.

Social representations are shared beliefs which are held by groups of people in society. Each of us adopts our own set of social representations, by talking with other people, picking ideas up from the mass media, and fitting these into our own personal construct system. They give us ways of explaining what is happening in our everyday experience. In some ways, they are a bit like personal constructs, but they are shared by other people too.

Among racists, a common social representation is the idea that they are somehow in competition with members of ethnic minorities for the benefits of society. So when those benefits become fewer, they blame the members of those ethnic groups.

SOCIAL IDENTIFICATION

Why should these people seize on members of a particular group, rather than on particular individuals? The answer to this question lies in the mechanism of social identification – a very basic tendency for human beings to see the world in terms of 'them' and 'us' groups. We are aware of the social groups and categories that we belong to, and we are also aware of other groups in society.

Because we tend to know the people in our own groups best, and we only see members of other groups from the outside, we become much more aware of the differences between people in our own group than we are of differences among others. So it is very easy for us to slip into the idea that 'we' are all different, whereas 'they' are all the same. One of the first steps in breaking down any sort of social prejudice is to recognize that any group of people is made up of individuals, with their own different ideas and opinions – that 'they' are not, in fact, all the same.

Another aspect of social identity theory is that we tend to make comparisons with people in groups which are close to us, socially and economically, because that way it helps us to feel good about belonging to our own group. Those racists who engage in violent action tend to be relatively less educated and to undertake unskilled work when they are employed. So, rather than place the blame for their unemployment on those in charge of the economy, who are socially very distant from them, they prefer to blame people who are in a similar economic position, but belong to a different social group.

MASLOW'S HIERARCHY OF NEEDS

Maslow suggested that it is useful to think of human motivation in terms of a hierarchy of needs (Figure 2). We have some needs which are absolutely basic – our physiological survival needs – and if these are not satisfied, they will motivate our behaviour almost completely. Our actions will be aimed towards getting food, drink, shelter from the elements and so on, and we will have little time for anything else. But once those needs are satisfied, a different layer in the hierarchy begins to become important. Each time one level of needs is satisfied, the next level becomes important as a motivator.

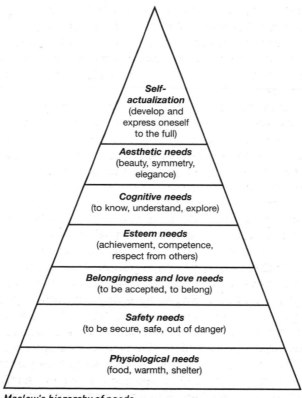

Figure 2 Maslow's hierarchy of needs

SUNDAY

MONDAY

TUESDAY

WEDNESDAY

THURSDAY

FRIDAY

SATURDAY

Maslow's theory may be sound as a general tendency, but there are numerous examples of people acting in ways which are quite different from what would be predicted by Maslow. What Maslow described as 'higher' needs are often extremely important to people – so much so that whether their basic needs have been satisfied sometimes doesn't come into it.

It is perhaps more useful, if we are trying to understand human motivation, to take an approach which looks at it in terms of levels of explanation, than to try to explain it as a hierarchy of needs. We all operate on different levels at the same time.

We may do something because it is approved of by our social group, but also because we want to do it personally and because we believe it will be good for us. Some of our motives are conscious and deliberate, while others are unconscious and we aren't even aware of them at the time. And most of the things that we do are stimulated by several motives, rather than just one at a time. By looking at the many different kinds of motives which people have for their behaviour, we can identify some of the influences which might be producing that behaviour at a given time.

SUMMARY

The motivations for our actions can sometimes be very simple; often, though, they can be difficult to unpick or seem hopelessly confused or ambivalent. Today we have looked at the broad categories of motivation that influence us – from the physiological (e.g. hunger) and behavioural (e.g. habits), through the cognitive (our thoughts, beliefs and ideas), to the social (e.g. our desire for esteem or approval). Models of motivation, such as Maslow's 'hierarchy of needs', while useful, tend to offer too simplistic a picture. Human motives are often mixed and what constitutes a 'basic' need may differ from person to person.

Perhaps the most important thing to remember is that we almost never do anything for just one reason. Almost everything that we do will be influenced by several different types of motive, ranging from simple physiological needs, such as to be active, through individual needs such as our need to make cognitive sense of our experience, to social needs such as our need for positive regard from other people – and all at the same time!

SUNDAY

MONDAY

TUESDAY

WEDNESDAY

THURSDAY

FRIDAY

SATURDAY

FACT-CHECK (ANSWERS AT THE BACK)

1. Which one of the following is *not* a physical motivation?
   a) Warmth ❑
   b) Thirst ❑
   c) Hunger ❑
   d) Security ❑

2. What is a personal construct?
   a) A self-build house ❑
   b) The theories we build up from experience to anticipate events ❑
   c) The attitudes we develop from childhood onward ❑
   d) None of the above ❑

3. Which of the following is *not* a cognitive motive?
   a) A personal construct ❑
   b) A defence mechanism ❑
   c) A habit ❑
   d) A self-efficacy belief ❑

4. Who first formulated the idea of the defence mechanism?
   a) Carl Jung ❑
   b) Anna Freud ❑
   c) Melanie Klein ❑
   d) Sigmund Freud ❑

5. What term describes the opposite of a self-efficacy belief?
   a) Learned helplessness ❑
   b) Positive self-efficacy belief ❑
   c) Low self-esteem ❑
   d) None of the above ❑

6. What did Harré consider to be a very basic human motivation?
   a) Thirst ❑
   b) Social justice ❑
   c) Social respect ❑
   d) Pleasure ❑

7. What are social representations?
   a) Stereotypes ❑
   b) Prejudices ❑
   c) People elected to represent communities ❑
   d) Shared beliefs held by a group of people ❑

8. How might we sum up the mechanism of social identification?
   a) 'Us' and 'Them' ❑
   b) 'Thee' and 'Thou' ❑
   c) 'You' and 'Non-you' ❑
   d) None of the above ❑

9. What is at the apex of Maslow's 'hierarchy of needs'?
   a) Self-realization ❑
   b) The Self ❑
   c) Self-activation ❑
   d) Self-actualization ❑

10. Which of the following kinds of need comes first in Maslow's hierarchy of needs?
   a) Physiological ❑
   b) Cognitive ❑
   c) Aesthetic ❑
   d) Esteem ❑

WEDNESDAY

Cognitive psychology

The human mind stores our experiences and expectations, so we can use our knowledge for new purposes, or in new contexts; but some problem-solving works best when we try to escape from established expectations. When assumptions become too generally accepted, they can produce disastrous decision-making. Perceptual set can affect or even distort our cognition by encouraging us to interpret ambiguous information in just one way. But everyday perception tends to work in an active cycle, with our expectations being modified by information from the real world.

Similarly, memory is also a much more active process than people realize. Our memories are shaped almost as much by our expectations and assumptions as by what actually happened. Memory for factual information can be enhanced by processing the material, but what appears important, and what connects with other things, will still be shaped by our own interests and thought habits.

THINKING

In the 1960s and 1970s, a number of psychologists investigated how human beings go about solving problems, and found that, often, we don't seem to do it particularly logically. There are a number of mental 'traps' that we fall into very easily. One of the most important of these is when we have expectations about what we are likely to find, and these expectations affect what we do. Expectations can mean that we develop what is known as a **mental set**, which is a state of being especially ready to think in certain ways.

Groupthink

Groupthink is another major discovery from psychologists exploring different aspects of thinking – although, unfortunately, our understanding of what it is and how it happens doesn't seem to stop politicians and others from doing it. Essentially, groupthink happens when a group of people have become so comfortable and certain that their own way of seeing the world is right that they ignore or dismiss any information which contradicts their ideas. This can lead, and has led, to absolutely disastrous decisions at times.

The symptoms of groupthink were documented by the American psychologist Irving Janis in the 1970s. They include a sense of invulnerability, in that the group feels secure and unlikely to be seriously threatened; self-censorship, as people who disagree or have doubts keep them to themselves rather than risk the scorn of others; rejecting undesirable information by stereotyping those who provide it or treating it as unacceptable; and, most importantly, maintaining an illusion of unanimity, because everyone is conforming to the majority view. Many psychologists see this as one of the best ways to diagnose groupthink. If everyone appears to agree with everyone else, then that's a sure sign either that someone is hiding something or that the group needs some fresh viewpoints.

Groupthink...

Sometimes, we can train our thinking so that it deliberately avoids being influenced by previous expectations and assumptions. In the 1960s, Edward de Bono developed a technique known as **lateral thinking**, in which people consciously learned to try to solve problems by thinking 'outside the box' – in other words, by ignoring the usual approaches and going at the problem from an entirely different angle.

Lateral solutions aren't always the right ones, of course; but being able to think laterally helps to increase the range of options that we see as available to us, and can often help us overcome tricky problems. A group-based form of lateral thinking has become very popular when people are looking for new ideas. It is known as **brainstorming**, and when it is done properly its first stage is for people to produce as many ideas as they possibly can, with nobody dismissing anything as impractical or unrealistic. After that, there is a second, separate stage where the ideas are evaluated. Having an open ideas session first can sometimes produce ideas which seem completely unrealistic at first sight, but actually prove to be workable and positive when they have been looked at thoroughly.

PERCEPTION

Perception is all about interpreting the information that the mind receives from the outside world, and working out what it means. The psychological study of perception involves looking at how the mind acts on the information it receives through the senses, to give us our perceptual experience.

PERCEPTUAL SET

Just as our experience gives us mental sets which influence how we think when we are solving problems, so expectation or mood, or other influences, can give us **perceptual sets**, which influence what we perceive. In one famous study, Bruner and Minturn (1955) showed people sets of letters or numbers. Each time they saw a letter or a number, they were asked to say what it was out loud. Then they were shown an ambiguous figure, which could be seen as either the figure 13 or the letter B. People who had previously been looking at letters said that it was a 'B', while people who had previously seen numbers said that it was a 13. Their prior experience had given them a perceptual set, which had affected their perception.

Perception can also be influenced by our physical or motivational state. Back in the 1950s, Gilchrist and Nesburg asked people to look at pictures and to rate how brightly coloured they were. Some pictures were of neutral stimuli, such as landscapes, while others were of food and drink. If the research participants had gone without food or drink for four hours or more, they saw pictures of food and drink as more brightly coloured than the other pictures. Their motivational state – hunger – had affected how they perceived the pictures.

THE PERCEPTUAL CYCLE

All this sounds as though we only see what we want or expect to see. That's partly true, but it isn't the whole story. Neisser (1976) described perception as taking place in a continuously active cycle. We begin with schemas that we use to make sense of the world. Those schemas help us to anticipate what we are likely to encounter, so Neisser referred to them as **anticipatory schemas**.

Our schemas direct what sorts of things we notice as we explore the perceptual world. We don't take in everything around us – if we did, we would soon become overloaded. We wouldn't know when to take notice of the shadow of a leaf, or the texture of the tarmac on a road, or anything else. So what we do is sample the relevant information. If we want to cross the road, we notice the speed of the car that is approaching, the width of the road and other bits of information which might be relevant to what we want to do, and we ignore the rest. We sample the perceptual world through our perceptual exploration and that in turn has been shaped by our anticipatory schemas.

Once we have sampled the information, it feeds back to the anticipatory schema and modifies it. You may have been about to step into the road because your anticipatory schema has to do with being on the other side, but your perceptual exploration led you to focus on approaching cars, and the information available told you that there was one coming up fast. So you modify your anticipatory schema, waiting until the car has gone past. The modified schema in turn directs a new set of perceptual exploration (looking further down the road to see how many more cars are coming), and so on.

In Neisser's model, then, perception is a continuous, active cycle, not just a passive snapshot of what is there. What we anticipate or expect to happen affects what we perceive; but what is actually there affects what we anticipate. So our expectations are continually changing and adjusting themselves as we take in new information and revise our schemas accordingly.

MEMORY

Memory, too, is an active mental process rather than a simple video-recording of what has happened. In many ways, this is quite a hard concept to grasp, because we always feel as though we are remembering exactly what happened. But it's true, nonetheless. The trouble, though, is that we don't often have a separate, objective record of what actually did happen, so we can't compare our memories with the real thing.

There are a few occasions when we do have some objective evidence to compare it with, though. Have you ever been to see a film twice, with a gap of several years in between? If you have, you will often find that some of your favourite scenes in the film don't happen exactly the way that you remember them. Even though you felt you remembered them word for word, they turn out to be different when you actually see them again.

This actually reflects a powerful feature of our memory, which has been known to psychologists for a very long time. Bartlett, in 1932, showed how, when people are asked to remember a story, they make sense of the story in their own way. We fit new information into our existing thought structures – into the schemas that we use for understanding the world. This often means that we unconsciously adjust the information so that it will fit our schema.

WORDS AND MEMORY

Memories can be influenced by all sorts of subtle factors. In a study described by Loftus and Loftus in 1975, people were shown a film of a traffic accident. They were then asked questions about it. Among the questions there was one about the speed of the cars, and this was phrased very carefully. Half of the people were asked 'How fast were the cars going when they hit one another?' while the other half were asked 'How fast were the cars going when they smashed into one another?' All the other questions were the same.

A week later, the same people were asked to remember the film they had seen. Among other things, they were asked whether there had been any broken glass in the film. There hadn't been any, and those who had been asked about the cars hitting one another remembered that. But those who had been asked about the cars smashing into one another distinctly remembered broken glass strewn around the road, and were surprised to find that it wasn't there when they saw the film again. The words which were used when they were asked about the accident had directly influenced what they remembered – to the point of introducing details which hadn't been there originally.

A false memory?

This is an important finding, particularly for people who have to ask questions of witnesses for court. People can pick up subtle hints and suggestions from the words that are used, and are often entirely unaware that they are doing it. In some US states, the police experimented with helping witnesses to remember what happened by using hypnosis, because they believed it would help people to recall events. But when people are hypnotized, they are even more easily influenced, and they are also trying very hard to be co-operative. Because of this, they often adjust their memories, without knowing it, to fit what they think the questioner wants to know.

As a result of this, Gibson (1982) argued that the use of hypnotism on witnesses in police investigations should be regarded as being equivalent to tampering with evidence. Memory doesn't work like a video-recording. It can be changed and adjusted even some time after the event, without the person even knowing. And once that has happened, there is no way at all of telling the difference between a constructed memory and a 'real' one.

A 'GOOD' MEMORY

You may have wondered what makes a good memory and why some people seem to have good memories while others don't. A very large part of that answer is to do with how we go about storing the information in the first place.

Whenever we store information, we process it in some way. We might, for instance, change something from a verbal form (words) into a visual form, such as a diagram or a picture. Or we might hear someone say something and store it in terms of the meaning of what they have said – linking it with other things which have similar meanings, and so on. All this is mental processing of the information.

In one classic study, Morris et al. (1981) asked people to remember a list of words and numbers – a single number attached to each word – which was read out to them. They had two groups of people participating in their study. One group was not particularly interested in what they were doing, but tried to remember the list anyway. The other group was really, deeply interested in it. When they were tested to see how many items from the list they could remember, the interested group remembered far more than the uninterested group.

The reason why they were so interested was because they were very keen football supporters, and this was Saturday afternoon. They had agreed to come along to the researcher's laboratory, and were hearing the results of that day's matches read out on the radio. So as they listened, they were thinking about each result, about how it fitted into the overall picture, and what difference it would make to that team's league position. In other words, they were processing the information. The others, who were not particularly keen on football, just listened and tried to remember, but they didn't process the information as much, which is why they didn't remember it as well.

So, if you want to try to improve your memory, there's the answer. Don't just try to remember things passively: process them. Change the form of the information in some way: use imagery to change it into pictures, or change it into symbols. Fit it into your schemas and concepts, by working out what it means and why it matters. You'll be surprised how much you can remember when you do that.

SUMMARY

Today we have seen how the mind easily gets into 'bad habits' or into 'a groove' and that this predisposes us to think, perceive and remember in a certain way. Far from thinking logically, we usually just think in the ways we have always thought (which we blithely call 'logical', but which can be quite the opposite at times). Furthermore, instead of remembering something objectively, as if we were some kind of walking camera, we actually recall information in a highly subjective and biased way. Such cognitive 'sets' can have important consequences, as seen in the varying testimonies in a courtroom or the collective follies of a bank.

There are ways of getting the brain to reset itself and to think and see in as fresh a way as possible. De Bono's lateral thinking is perhaps one of the best-known examples of such brain-training techniques. We can also improve our memories quite dramatically by working with information to make it personally relevant.

SUNDAY

MONDAY

TUESDAY

WEDNESDAY

THURSDAY

FRIDAY

SATURDAY

FACT-CHECK (ANSWERS AT THE BACK)

1. Typically, humans think...
   a) In an entirely logical way ❑
   b) Objectively ❑
   c) With a set of expectations already in place ❑
   d) Irrationally ❑

2. What brain-training technique did Edward de Bono pioneer?
   a) Oblique thinking ❑
   b) Lateral thinking ❑
   c) Organic thinking ❑
   d) Brainstorming ❑

3. What is groupthink? Where a group of people...
   a) Have got into the habit of thinking in a certain way ❑
   b) Are certain they are always right ❑
   c) Refuse to see ideas and arguments that don't fit in with their way of doing things ❑
   d) All of the above ❑

4. Which of the following are examples of perceptual set?
   a) 12 B 14 ❑
   b) The cat sat on the map ❑
   c) Perceiving a photograph of a cake as more brightly coloured when you are hungry ❑
   d) All of the above ❑

5. An anticipatory schema...
   a) Helps us to deal with past traumas ❑
   b) Is used only when crossing the road ❑
   c) Helps us to anticipate what we are likely to encounter ❑
   d) Is a term coined by Gilchrist and Nesburg ❑

6. How might we sum up Neisser's model of perception?
   a) Passive ❑
   b) Active ❑
   c) Fixed ❑
   d) Retrospective ❑

7. Which of the following describes psychologists' understanding of the memory?
   a) Accurate ❑
   b) Constructive ❑
   c) Physiological ❑
   d) Concurrent ❑

8. Memory recall can be coloured by...
   a) Words ❑
   b) Emotions ❑
   c) Time ❑
   d) All of the above ❑

9. According to Gibson, hypnotism isn't a good technique to use on witnesses because...
   a) It makes them sleepy ❑
   b) Memories can be tampered with ❑
   c) It makes them forgetful ❑
   d) None of the above ❑

10. Which of the following are good memory-boosting techniques?
    a) Changing information into icons or mental images ❑
    b) Learning to recite your favourite poem off by heart ❑
    c) Copying out notes ❑
    d) Learning the telephone directory ❑

THURSDAY

Evolution and genetics

Evolutionary processes include natural selection and the principles of biodiversity and co-evolution. Although simplistic similarities have been drawn with other animals, the key in human evolution is our adaptability, partly shaped by our bodies and partly by our sociability.

Evolution occurs through small changes in genetic transmission. But our genes do not entirely determine who we are: the environment we live in affects which genes will be influential in our personal development.

Animals, including humans, have also evolved the capacity for basic learning, particularly in terms of maximizing their survival. Foods which make us sick may be poisonous, so just one experience will make us (and other animals) avoid them. This is known as one-trial learning. There are other forms of animal learning, too. However, most human learning is at a more complex level. We'll look at this tomorrow.

MAN AND BEAST

Human beings have learned to live in almost all parts of the world, under wildly different physical conditions. That learning is only possible because we have evolved such a large amount of flexibility and adaptability in both our brains and our immune systems. Looking at how brains and learning capacities have developed in other animals can help us to understand more about how we came to be the way we are.

But we need to be cautious when we are trying to generalize from other animals to human beings. This is because of the very diverse ways that other animals have evolved. Nature may use the same materials but in very different ways. Some studies of animal physiology, for example, have shown that the same brain chemical, in apparently the same part of the brain, can produce completely different behaviours in rats and cats – behaviours as different as sleeping and aggression. Animal social organization varies widely, sometimes even in the same species – for example, plains baboons have a much more rigid social hierarchy than forest baboons, which are more relaxed and 'egalitarian' in their relationships with one another. So we should be very careful when making comparisons.

Comparative psychology is firmly based on the idea that all animals, including human beings, have evolved from primitive common ancestors. The **theory of evolution**, as put forward by Charles Darwin in 1859, proposes that different animal species have changed and developed continuously over time, as they become better suited to their environments. Evolution happens through small genetic changes as the species gradually adapts to the demands and rigours of the environment that it lives in.

NATURAL SELECTION

Individuals result from a combination of biological inheritance and environmental experiences. Both genetics and the environment work together, each making it possible for the other to have its influence. Humans, for example, learn from their environments all the time. But without the human brain, which has developed as a result of genetic factors, that learning would be totally impossible. And without its earlier environment and pressures, the human brain would not have taken that particular form in the first place.

Natural selection – the basis of evolution – works by 'shaping' the set of genes that are inherited from the parents. Each of us is unique, and the same applies in other species as well as humans. Sometimes the combination of genes that an individual inherits is particularly beneficial. As a result, and given the right environment, the individual may be stronger, or healthier, than others of its kind. And, because it is a little bit healthier, it will also be more likely to reproduce successfully, so its beneficial mutation can be passed on to future generations.

Natural selection!

One of the 'classic' examples of evolution is that of the finches on the Galapagos Islands. When Darwin reached these islands, on the voyage made by the famous ship HMS *Beagle*, each island had a slightly different kind of finch living on it. However, when he examined the different finches, it was apparent that, at some time in the past, they had all developed from just one species. That species had originally colonized all the islands. But because each island presented a slightly different environment, natural selection meant that the birds had gradually adapted to their particular island. In the process, they had become different from the finches on the other islands.

This continuous process of adaptation and development has produced a vast diversity of living organisms, ranging from plants and yeasts to mammals and birds.

The principle of **biodiversity** means that there are examples of almost every different kind of activity that we can think of somewhere in the animal kingdom. In many species, for instance, it is the fathers which rear the young rather than the mothers – after all, they too have invested their genes in their offspring. In some species, males hold territories; in others, females do. The more we look, the more variation we find.

Co-evolution

Evolution isn't just a one-way process. Even an amoeba, which has only one body cell, secretes chemicals into the water that it swims in, and so changes that water. And more complex animals often exert quite a strong influence over their environments, so that the environments also evolve with the animals.

This process is known as **co-evolution** and it is something which is often overlooked when people talk about evolutionary processes. Animals don't just adapt to their environments; environments also adapt to their animals. And, sometimes, animals shape their environments so that they will fit their needs better. It is this two-way relationship which we need to bear in mind when we are looking at human psychological processes and evolution.

GENETIC MECHANISMS

Evolution is determined by the genes that we inherit from our parents. In recent years we have come to understand a great deal more about how this works, and that has helped us to understand quite a lot about individual differences.

When we, or any other living things, reproduce ourselves sexually – that is, by combining sperm from one parent with ova from another – we do it by producing special cells which only have half of the chromosomes: one from each pair.

These combine with the cells from the other parent to form a complete set, which can then develop into a new individual. In this way, the new individual inherits some characteristics from each of its parents, and that mixture is slightly different every time. These characteristics are contained as DNA in the chromosomes. But another kind of DNA – mitochondrial DNA – is contained in the cells of the host mother, who is providing the environment for the new organism to develop.

So from the moment that the embryo begins to develop – in other words, from the moment of conception – there is a continual interaction between the two types of DNA and the environment in which the individual is developing.

Factors such as the amount of oxygen or nutrients available, the presence of stress hormones or drugs, and the amount of activity of the mother all have an influence on the embryo's development in the womb or the egg; and these environmental factors continue and become even more significant throughout the whole of an individual's development. Someone who has only a restricted diet when they are young, for example, may not develop the full height and bone size that they might have had with a richer diet.

The total set of genetic characteristics that we inherit is known as the **genotype** – but nobody ever sees a genotype in real life. What we actually see, in any animal, plant or human being, is the **phenotype** – what has actually developed as a result of the interaction between the genes and the environment.

That's an important thing to know, because it tells us that genetic influences are not fixed and inevitable. Genetic influences predispose us towards certain types of development. But the environment can make a tremendous difference. Some people have inherited a genetic tendency towards heart disease, which means that with certain kinds of environmental stressors, they are likely to develop it. But if they know that they carry the gene, then they can develop a lifestyle which will help them to avoid the illness – by keeping to a healthy diet, taking regular exercise and so on. Having a genetic tendency to something doesn't make it inevitable. It just means we are more vulnerable and so we need to take precautions.

SUNDAY

MONDAY

TUESDAY

WEDNESDAY

THURSDAY

FRIDAY

SATURDAY

LEARNING

Just about all types of animal are capable of some kind of learning – even those with very primitive nervous systems. But each species is predisposed towards the types of learning which are most appropriate for the environment in which they live. Bees, for example, can easily learn from smells or colours, but not from sounds. In this way, genes can facilitate learning by making some kinds of learning easier than others, for that particular species.

Perhaps the most basic type of learning is pain avoidance. Even a flatworm, which has a very primitive, ladder-like nervous system, can learn to turn in a particular direction if turning the other way brings it into contact with a painful stimulus. That kind of learning happens at a very simple level, in the connections made directly by the nerve cells; and, as you can imagine, it is an important mechanism to help the animal survive.

ONE-TRIAL LEARNING AND IMPRINTING

Some kinds of learning are closely directed by genetic mechanisms. One of the best examples is the way that we avoid foods which have made us sick. This is a useful mechanism to evolve, since in the natural world something which makes you sick is likely to be poisonous, so learning to avoid that food helps an individual to survive. It is an example of what is known as **one-trial learning** – a form of learning which is so powerful that we need only one connection between the stimulus and response to make it stick. Avoiding foods that have made you sick in the past isn't confined to humans – it's something that most animals will do. Both human beings and animals can have an inherited predisposition to learn some things very quickly indeed.

Another very rapid form of learning is shown by some precocial animals soon after they are born. Precocial animals are ones which can move around very soon after birth, such as foals or lambs, ducklings and goslings. If they didn't learn quickly how to recognize their mothers and stick with them, they'd be at risk of wandering off and getting eaten by predators. So they have a very rapid form of learning, known as **imprinting**, whereby they develop an attachment and follow the object of their attachment around in the first few hours after birth. With young goslings and ducklings, it seems to be mostly visual, in that they will imprint on the first large, moving object that they see, but with lambs the sense of smell and hearing also seems to be important. Whatever the mechanism, it is a fast, almost irreversible form of learning which has tremendous survival value.

GENERAL LEARNING

Learning, though, isn't only about linking one stimulus with a response. Some animals have inherited a predisposition for a more general kind of learning. They will explore places, or be curious about new objects. And sometimes, too, they seem to be ready to learn entirely new forms of behaviour.

Some animals can learn entirely new forms of behaviour

Rats and monkeys, for example, will generally explore new situations and investigate strange objects that they come across – unless there is some good reason to avoid them. And this exploration, too, can be an evolutionary advantage.

If you know that you are in a place with no escape, then the best thing to do is to try not to attract a predator's attention. If you don't know, then the best thing to do is to try to find a way out. But it is better to know, so exploring new places is a good way of surviving.

INHERITING THE BRAIN

The cerebrum of the brain is much larger and more highly developed in some species than it is in others. This is the part of the brain which we use for learning and thinking, and those animals which have the largest and most highly developed cerebrum also seem to be those animals which are most able to take advantage of opportunities for learning. As far as land animals are concerned, human beings have the most highly developed cerebrum of all. And we are also capable of learning more than any other land animals.

Human beings live in all kinds of conditions, from arctic wastes to tropical forests, so it would be inappropriate for us to be genetically prepared to deal with a particular physical environment. Instead, we are genetically prepared to interact with and learn from other human beings, and that's what allows us to survive.

Human learning, then, includes association learning and the basic survival mechanisms. But it encompasses much more than that. Our heritage as adaptable social animals means that we are engaging in social learning almost from birth: belonging to social groups is a significant motivator for human beings, and 'how to belong' is one of the most important forms of learning that we do. Our intrinsic ability to use and develop language means that we are able to pass on learning culturally, from one generation to another. And we also have a capacity for abstract thought and reasoning, which results in the more formal kinds of learning.

SUMMARY

Today we have looked at how comparative psychology can throw light on the development of the human brain and its capacities. In all animals, including humans, we have learned how both genetic and environmental factors have contributed to their evolution, and how, by looking at the development of other animals' brains, we can understand more about human beings'. We have, however, also looked at the limitations of comparative psychology: non-human animal physiology and behaviours are often very remote from their human counterparts.

At the heart of comparative psychology is the question of how animals, humans included, learn. Human learning, like other animal learning, includes association learning and the basic survival mechanisms. But it encompasses much more than that. As adaptable social animals we are engaging in social learning almost from birth: belonging to social groups is a significant motivator for human beings, and 'how to belong' is one of the most important forms of learning that we do.

SUNDAY

MONDAY

TUESDAY

WEDNESDAY

THURSDAY

FRIDAY

SATURDAY

FACT-CHECK (ANSWERS AT THE BACK)

1. Comparative psychology compares...
   a) Individual humans' brains ❑
   b) Humans with other animals ❑
   c) The development of the brain over time ❑
   d) None of the above ❑

2. For which of the following reasons is it necessary to be cautious when generalizing from other animals to human beings?
   a) Animal physiology can be very different ❑
   b) Not all animals are the same ❑
   c) Animal social organization can be very different ❑
   d) All of the above ❑

3. Evolution results from...
   a) A series of small genetic changes over generations ❑
   b) Animals and people learning to change their behaviour ❑
   c) The discovery of dinosaur fossils ❑
   d) Avoiding food that makes you sick ❑

4. What is co-evolution?
   a) The evolution of a biome ❑
   b) The evolution of a species ❑
   c) The mutual influence of animals and environment ❑
   d) None of the above ❑

5. What is a genotype?
   a) The ideal form of a species ❑
   b) The observable inherited characteristics of an organism ❑
   c) The total set of inherited characteristics of an organism ❑
   d) None of the above ❑

6. What is the phenotype?
   a) The ideal form of a species ❑
   b) The observable inherited characteristics of an organism ❑
   c) The total set of inherited characteristics of an organism ❑
   d) None of the above ❑

7. What of the following is a consequence of imprinting?
   a) A new-born calf sticking close to its mother ❑
   b) A chick hatching from its egg ❑
   c) A cat avoiding rotten food ❑
   d) A new-born lamb suckling ❑

8. General learning is about...
   a) Linking a stimulus with a response ❑
   b) Avoiding food that makes you sick ❑
   c) Learning about overall patterns or situations ❑
   d) Attaching rapidly to a parent ❑

9. What is the cerebrum? The part of the brain used for...
   a) Emotional reactions ❑
   b) Involuntary movement ❑
   c) Thinking ❑
   d) All of the above ❑

10. In humans, social learning begins...
   a) In nursery school/preschool ❑
   b) At birth or even before ❑
   c) At six months ❑
   d) At around five years ❑

FRIDAY

Learning and intelligence

Learning takes many forms, from basic conditioning to sophisticated social or cognitive analysis. Conditioning has two general forms: classical conditioning, which works by linking a stimulus and a response, and operant conditioning, which works by rewarding the correct response. But humans have other learning mechanisms too. Babies and children are particularly ready to use social learning mechanisms, like imitation. We also spend much of our lives learning or perfecting both mental and physical skills. All skills are learned through practice, which automatizes our actions, whether they are mental or physical, so that they become fluent and adaptable.

For modern psychologists, cognitive skills form the basis of what we know as intelligence. Rather than being a single 'thing', intelligence is now recognized as consisting of many different skills and abilities, with every human being having their strengths and weaknesses. Emotional intelligence, or sensitivity to others, is also recognized nowadays as a distinct set of mental abilities.

TYPES OF LEARNING
CONDITIONING

One of the most basic forms of learning, and one which is shared by other animals too, is known as association learning. Association learning is sometimes called **conditioning**, on the grounds that it is all about producing a particular response under particular conditions. It isn't really a 'thinking' type of learning at all. Instead, it is where we have learned to make an automatic response to some outside event or stimulus.

Classical conditioning, as studied by Ivan Pavlov, is the purest form of association learning and also seems to be the most primitive kind of learning of all. Pavlov studied dogs, and showed that their salivary reflex, which they produce automatically when they receive food, could be conditioned to take place when they heard a bell or a buzzer.

The other main type of association learning is known as **operant conditioning**. In this type of conditioning, we learn something because it is immediately followed by a pleasant effect. That pleasant effect is sometimes a direct reward. For example, a squirrel will learn to climb a washing-line pole to reach a bird-feeding tray and gain the food. Sometimes, though, the pleasant effect comes from the removal of something unpleasant. An animal might learn to press a lever in order to avoid receiving an electric shock; or a schoolgirl might do her homework purely in order to avoid getting into trouble the next day.

These two types of pleasant effect are both known as reinforcement – because they reinforce, or strengthen, the behaviour that we have learned. The kind where we receive a reward is called **positive reinforcement**, whereas the kind where we escape from, or avoid, something unpleasant is known as **negative reinforcement**. Both positive and negative reinforcement have to happen immediately after the particular action which is being learned. Conditioning doesn't work if they happen later – if we do learn from delayed rewards, it is a different type of learning.

Punishment is a bad way of training...

The psychologist who became known as the 'father' of operant conditioning, B.F. Skinner, insisted that punishment was a very bad way of training children – or animals for that matter – because it didn't give them any idea of what they ought to be doing instead. Skinner believed it was better to train children using operant conditioning, so they were rewarded for doing the right thing.

SOCIAL LEARNING

From its very earliest days, a young infant is learning to handle its world. Human infants are predisposed to react most strongly to other people, and learning from others is an important part of how the infant continues to develop.

SUNDAY

MONDAY

TUESDAY

WEDNESDAY

THURSDAY

FRIDAY

SATURDAY

Conditioning and society

In 1972 Skinner went on to argue that society as a whole should develop systematic ways of conditioning people into behaving appropriately. His book was called *Beyond Freedom and Dignity*, because he was arguing that there was no such thing as 'freedom' or 'dignity' – they were just an illusion, and all human behaviour was really shaped by conditioning.

Other psychologists, and people from other professions too, disagreed. They argued that people do have free will and are able to make real choices. There are other levels of learning and, as adaptable social animals, we do a great deal of learning directly from other people.

Imitation is an important form of learning because it is a kind of shortcut. If we learned everything through operant and classical conditioning, we would have to do everything by trial and error – doing it, and seeing what the consequences are. But life is too short for that. Using imitation, we can learn much more quickly.

Albert Bandura performed a number of studies in the 1970s, showing how people learn through imitation, and whom they are most likely to imitate. He found that children were most likely to imitate models like themselves – other children in preference to adults, people of the same gender and so on. They were also more likely to imitate people that they admired.

The most important finding of all was that what the children had learned didn't necessarily show up straight away. It remained latent, until it was needed. A child could see someone acting aggressively, and not seem to copy it at all. But later, if the child was in a situation where acting aggressively looked as though it would be useful, the child would act out the behaviour it had learned. Children store what they have learned, and use it only when the time seems right.

Schemas are an important way that human beings learn. We fit new experiences into what we already know and try to make sense of them that way. Sometimes, we are successful, and the new experience fits into our existing schemas, without anything needing to change much. That learning process is known as **assimilation** – where an existing schema is applied to a new situation.

Sometimes, though, our new experience doesn't fit into our previous schemas very well. When this happens, the schema has to change, as it adjusts itself to the new information. This is known as **accommodation**. Some psychologists and educationalists see accommodation as being the basis of all cognitive learning: we develop our understanding by extending and adjusting our existing ideas.

SKILL LEARNING

Not all types of learning are to do with absorbing new information. A great deal of the learning that we do is concerned with learning skills – both physical skills and mental ones.

All skills are different, but they all have one thing in common. That is, that the individual units of the skill have become automatized. The person does them automatically, without thinking about it. Because they don't have to think about specific actions, this leaves the person free to concentrate on other aspects of what they are doing – such as thinking about their complete performance in a music exam, or the meaning of the story they are reading, or the best route to take.

Skills become automatized through practice. The more we do a set of actions, the more likely we are to link those actions into a complete, fluent movement that we don't have to think about. We can automatize mental abilities as well as physical actions: not only reading but other mental abilities, too, such as the ability to do arithmetical calculations or to recognize patterns. With enough practice, people can become fluent in many different mental skills. And it is generalized mental skills which we are talking of when we talk about the human quality known as intelligence.

Practice makes perfect!

INTELLIGENCE

Intelligence is a difficult thing to define. Although psychologists use intelligence tests sometimes, this is not because they measure the limit of our intelligence (you can get better at intelligence tests if you practise them) but because they can help us to know a bit more about that person. Intelligence tests may not tell us exactly how intelligent someone is, but they do tell us how well developed certain of their skills are.

Gardner (1986) proposed that there isn't a single thing called intelligence, but that what we are actually referring to is a set of seven entirely different intelligences. The seven types of intelligence are outlined in Table 2.

Table 2 Gardner's seven intelligences

Intelligence	Description
Linguistic intelligence	– to do with language and how we use it
Musical intelligence	– to do with musical appreciation as well as performing and composing music
Mathematical-logical intelligence	– to do with calculation and logical reasoning
Spatial intelligence	– to do with art and design, as well as finding your way around
Bodily kinaesthetic intelligence	– to do with physical skills, like sport, dancing and other aspects of movement
Interpersonal intelligence	– to do with interacting with people socially and sensitively
Intrapersonal intelligence	– to do with understanding your own personal self and abilities

Each of these types, according to Gardner, is completely separate. Most people that we would call 'intelligent' have a combination of these different abilities, but some are particularly good at only one or two, and not at the others. A musical genius, for instance, will have one type of intelligence very highly developed, but might be quite ordinary in other respects. What we call an 'idiot savant' is someone who is well below average intelligence in most respects, but has one outstanding ability – to remember, or to calculate. Gardner's idea of separate intelligences shows how this may be possible.

One problem with Gardner's approach, though, is that it tends to treat these separate intelligences as if they just developed within the person, and have nothing to do with social influences. Although he drew much of his evidence from the biographies of high-achieving people, Gardner ignored the social influences on them. But people who achieve outstanding ability in any area have usually had at least one person who believed in them and encouraged them. Some psychologists believe that this influence may be more important than we realize.

Emotional intelligence

Another form of intelligence is all to do with maintaining positive interactions and relationships with other people. Some people are noticeably better at this than others. They show more social understanding, are more likely to spot when someone is distressed or upset, are more diplomatic in how they say things and generally more sensitive to social demands. These people have higher levels of **emotional intelligence**, and this is another quality which makes a considerable difference in everyday life.

SUMMARY

Today's chapter has been concerned with human learning – how we acquire, or modify, knowledge, behaviours, skills and so on. Once again, we have discovered that this a far more complicated process (or rather set of processes) than at first appears. Broadly, however, we have looked at three major kinds of learning: association learning (which is the 'automatic' kind of learning), social learning (learning acquired from our interactions with other people) and skill learning (which occurs through practice).

We use all three kinds of learning throughout our lives, though each may take on a greater prominence at various life stages or within different contexts – a new-born baby will be more engaged in the association and social types of learning, while an apprentice plumber will be concentrating on acquiring his or her new skill.

SUNDAY

MONDAY

TUESDAY

WEDNESDAY

THURSDAY

FRIDAY

SATURDAY

FACT-CHECK (ANSWERS AT THE BACK)

1. Which of these is not an example of associative learning?
a) One-trial learning ❏
b) Avoidance learning ❏
c) Conditioning ❏
d) Imitation ❏

2. Which scientist is most strongly associated with classical conditioning?
a) Charles Darwin ❏
b) Ivan Pavlov ❏
c) B.F. Skinner ❏
d) None of the above ❏

3. What is operant conditioning?
a) Learning by practice ❏
b) Learning by reflex ❏
c) Learning by reward ❏
d) Learning by social interaction ❏

4. What are the two types of reinforcement?
a) Light and heavy ❏
b) Positive and negative ❏
c) Right and wrong ❏
d) Inwards and outwards ❏

5. Who is known as the 'father' of operant conditioning?
a) B.F. Skinner ❏
b) Ivan Pavlov ❏
c) Howard Gardner ❏
d) None of the above ❏

6. How might we best sum up Skinner's idea?
a) Conditioning fails to account for human behaviour ❏
b) Conditioning accounts for around 50 per cent of human behaviour ❏
c) Conditioning is vital for human happiness ❏
d) All human behaviour is shaped by conditioning ❏

7. Imitation is a type of...
a) Associative learning ❏
b) Social learning ❏
c) Skill learning ❏
d) None of the above ❏

8. Bandura found that children are most likely to imitate...
a) People they see in the media ❏
b) People they admire ❏
c) People of the same sex ❏
d) People like them ❏

9. What do we call 'a learned ability that has become automatic through practice'?
a) Knowledge ❏
b) A skill ❏
c) A craft ❏
d) An art ❏

10. How many types of intelligence are there, according to Gardner?
a) Just one ❏
b) None – it doesn't exist! ❏
c) Seven ❏
d) Six ❏

SATURDAY

From
childhood to
old age

Each phase of life presents its own psychological challenges and conflicts which may need to be resolved.

As human beings, we have an extended period of childhood, which allows us to learn appropriate social behaviour. Interacting with siblings or other children can help pre-schoolers to develop the emotional skills that they will need in the future, but adult influence and support are important if children are to develop qualities such as achievement motivation or high self-efficacy beliefs.

Adolescence is a time of change and transition for young people, with an increasing number of social roles and responsibilities, but it is not inevitably turbulent.

We don't stop developing when we reach adulthood. People pass through a number of transitions during the course of their lives, and different periods of our lives bring different challenges and require different skills. As our understanding of lifespan psychology improves, we increasingly recognize how important it is to have the opportunity for a constructive and pleasant retirement.

CHILDHOOD

In the 1980s, a group of researchers based at Cambridge University explored how small children interact at home, and found that children are far more socially competent than they had thought. The child doesn't just pick up what it is supposed to do from praise or punishment – it takes part, actively, in a series of dynamic and emotional exchanges.

Some of those exchanges consisted of **teasing** older brothers or sisters. Children often deliberately provoke their siblings, sometimes to the point of tears. Every family is different, and some families quarrel more than others; but teasing is a very common activity among preschool children, and one which they become more sophisticated at as they grow older. Up until the age of about two, the child tends only to tease its older or younger siblings; but from age two onwards, it is just as likely to tease its mother – often by deliberately beginning to do something forbidden while she is watching, and seeing how she reacts.

Children don't just tease, though; they also try to comfort their siblings, and even their parents, when they are upset. Even children as young as two years old will respond to a brother or sister's distress, and try to comfort him or her by offering toys or stroking. Comforting was particularly evident among the older pre-school children in the Cambridge study. By 14 months or so, younger children will also comfort their older brothers and sisters when they are upset, or their parents when they have accidents or minor upsets.

By and large, a child becomes fully aware of other people as independent individuals, with minds and feelings of their own, at around the age of three and a half. This awareness is the basis for empathy, social responsibility and all sorts of other qualities which are such an important part of belonging to society – and we acquire it far earlier in life than researchers used to think.

SOCIAL INFLUENCE

Children continue to develop throughout their childhood. Their learning is structured by school, by parenting, and by other social interactions that the child experiences. The Russian child psychologist Lev Vygotsky emphasized the importance of other people in the child's cognitive development, and argued that their influence is essential if a child is to realize its full cognitive potential.

The **zone of proximal development**, according to Vygotsky, is that part of the child's potential which the child is able to achieve with structure and guidance from others. This is far greater than a child can manage on its own, as parents and teachers know intuitively. It includes abstract thinking, reasoning, problem-solving, complex language use and the development of sophisticated memorizing. All of these are cognitive abilities which are brought on and developed by the child's school and family experiences – the informal teaching which happens in families, schools and neighbourhoods is just as important for the child's cognitive development as formal teaching in school.

As any teacher will tell you, some children seem to have a much stronger need for achievement than others. These children often learn well, because success is important to them and so they put a great deal of effort into studying. It is helpful for children to have a reasonably high level of **achievement motivation**, because this will see them through temporary difficulties and setbacks as they come to terms with new things.

In one early study, Bernard Rosen and Roy D'Andrade (1959) showed that children with the highest level of achievement motivation had parents who consistently gave them praise and encouragement. Their parents also had quite high expectations – they anticipated that their child would do quite well in the task, and the children often lived up to those expectations. Parents of children with low achievement motivation didn't expect their children to achieve very much, and didn't particularly encourage them either.

SCHEMA DEVELOPMENT

The great child psychologist Jean Piaget developed a theory of the child's cognitive development, which detailed the mental skills which children acquire at different stages in their development. Piaget believed that young children are fundamentally egocentric – that is, they are entirely driven by their own experiences, and are unable to conceptualize abstract concepts or ideas outside their own experience. This egocentricity decreases gradually through childhood, as the child develops cognitive schemas which it uses to make sense of the world.

Schemas are mental structures which organize the child's knowledge, and they grow and develop from each other. The very first experiences of the world become gradually organized by the young infant into 'me' and 'not me'– the beginnings of the body-schema. As the child grows, these schemas develop and become more sophisticated through two processes: assimilation, in which new experiences are absorbed into the schema so that it can be used more widely; and accommodation, in which the schema itself is stretched, or even divided, to fit the new experiences.

There has been a great deal of controversy about Piaget's stages – many psychologists nowadays feel that they over-simplified what the child was capable of, and that they also ignored the child's social competences. One of the main problems was Piaget's insistence that children were simply not capable of certain kinds of operations until they reached

Table 2 Piagetian stages

Stage	Age (approx)	Description
The sensorimotor stage	0–2 years	Learning to organize and interpret sensory information and to co-ordinate motor activity.
The pre-operational stage	2–7 years	Beginning to reduce egocentricity, but can only take account of one feature at a time in conservation problems, and is unable to decentre.
The concrete operational stage	7–11 years	Able to undertake adult-style cognitive operations; but only with real-world targets.
The formal operational stage	11+	The child is now fully decentred, and can undertake abstract reasoning and perform logical operations.

certain ages. Many researchers since have shown that the tasks which Piaget used were only difficult for children because they were taken out of context and presented to them in an abstract way.

ADOLESCENCE

As the child's body matures, the child begins to enter adolescence. Adolescence is often thought of as a turbulent period – a period of upheaval and rebellion from parental authority. This image of adolescence has been very popular with Hollywood since the 1950s, and it has passed into our everyday consciousness.

Some anthropologists and psychologists, such as Margaret Mead and Urie Bronfenbrenner, argued that it arose as a result of the alienation of young people from adult culture in Western capitalist societies. In non-technological societies, Mead argued, adolescents were fully participating members of their communities, and so were not left to their own devices and regarded as a separate culture. Even in Soviet Russia, Bronfenbrenner argued, young people were more integrated into their society than they were in the USA, and showed fewer signs of alienation.

All of these theorists, however, were working on the assumption that a turbulent adolescence was the normal state of affairs for young people in Western societies. But gradually this view was challenged as psychologists such as Albert Bandura began to study 'normal' adolescents, rather than adolescents who were attending clinics or courts because they were disturbed or troublesome. Bandura found that most adolescents don't particularly oppose their parents' values or show rebellion. Rather, for many people, adolescence is a period in which they develop a more trusting and positive relationship with their parents, rather than the reverse.

Adolescence can be seen as a period of role transition – a time when teenagers are changing how they interact with society in general, and with the other people around them. Moving from school to work, or from school to higher education, involves adopting different social roles, and

SUNDAY

MONDAY

TUESDAY

WEDNESDAY

THURSDAY

FRIDAY

SATURDAY

these in turn can produce changes as different sides of the personality emerge.

Part of being an adolescent involves balancing out the different demands of the social roles that we are called on to play. Sometimes these result in widely differing expectations: someone might be regarded as a responsible adult in their Saturday job, as a child by members of their family, and as an irresponsible teenager by their schoolteacher. Each of these expectations will bring different 'selves', or aspects of the personality, to the fore, so balancing their different demands is something which takes a bit of learning.

Erik Erikson identified a number of different conflicts which each individual has to resolve as they pass through life. These are listed in Table 3. The successful resolution of early conflicts set the foundation for the later ones, so all the stages are important in the person's psychological development.

The particular conflict which needs to be resolved during adolescence is that of identity versus role confusion. Erikson saw it as important that the adolescent could accept that they had a single, integrated identity, despite the fact that they played so many social roles and acted differently in each one.

Gould (1978) developed the idea that adult life consists of a series of **transitions**, or life changes, which occur at different times in our lives. The first of these is that of adjusting to the responsibilities of being independent and living away from parental care.

This transition, Gould argued, takes place usually between the ages of 16 and 22. Then there is another transition, which takes place during our twenties, in which we develop our own competences and autonomy, and choose our own rules to live by, rather than simply conforming to our parents' rules and principles. A third transition, according to Gould, happens between 28 and 34, as we come to know ourselves better, and learn to come to terms with aspects of our nature which we weren't really aware of before. And the final transition involves accepting that life isn't going to last for ever – that is, developing a sense of our own mortality. This final transition, Gould argued, happens between the ages of 35 and 45.

Table 3 Erikson's stages of lifespan development

Early infancy	**Trust vs mistrust** The infant has to strike a balance between trusting people and risking disappointment, or being mistrustful and unable to relate to other people fully.
Later infancy	**Autonomy vs shame and doubt** The toddler has to develop a sense of personal agency and control over its behaviour and actions, rather than mistrusting its ability to do things.
Early childhood	**Initiative vs guilt** The child has to develop an increasing sense of personal responsibility and initiative, rather than simply feeling guilty and uncertain.
Middle childhood	**Industry vs inferiority** The child has to learn that systematic effort will overcome challenges, rather than just giving up and accepting failure.
Puberty and adolescence	**Identity vs role confusion** The adolescent needs to develop a consistent sense of inner self, rather than being swamped by the range of roles and choices available.
Young adulthood	**Intimacy vs isolation** The young adult needs to learn to develop intimate and trusting relationships with others, rather than avoiding relationships because they can become threatening and painful.
Mature adulthood	**Generativity vs stagnation** The adult needs to develop a productive life, recognizing their personal achievements and abilities, instead of stagnating psychologically.
Late adulthood	**Integrity vs despair** The older person needs to be able to look back on their life positively, rather than to feel that it has been meaningless and futile.

THE MID-LIFE CRISIS

One of the more popular ideas in recent years is that of the **mid-life crisis**. Temporary work, redundancies, adult retraining schemes and a greater emphasis on job satisfaction mean that many people hit a period in their forties or fifties when they begin to re-evaluate their lives, and decide that they want to do something which is more personally meaningful for them.

Sometimes this crisis simply takes the form of the person looking for a different job. But in the modern world, such decisions usually mean retraining, and some people go back into full-time education to achieve this. Universities have growing numbers of adult students, as do colleges and training schemes, and even people who left school feeling that they were too 'thick' to gain qualifications find that this is not so, and that they can learn as effectively as anyone else.

Other people may make more dramatic changes in their lives – perhaps moving to start a new life in a different country, or a different town, and taking up an entirely new occupation. Making such dramatic changes sometimes doesn't work very well, but often people report increased feelings of well-being and confidence, and more positive life experiences. As we have seen, we continue to grow and develop throughout our lives, and the mid-life crisis can be seen as a way of taking control of that growth and channelling it into new directions.

RETIREMENT

Another major transition, of course, is **retirement**. In earlier times, the period of retirement used to be a brief interlude before old age and death. But in modern living, it has become quite different. Changes in diet, lifestyle and general health mean that most people continue to live an active, productive life for a long period after they finish formal working – as long as 30 or 40 years. This period is very nearly as long as many people's working life, so the idea of retirement as a 'restful interlude' isn't really very practical. Instead, lifespan psychologists nowadays see retirement as a way of developing in new and different ways.

Organizations like the University of the Third Age encourage retired people to develop new hobbies and pursue new interests, and are becoming more popular and successful all the time. Many psychologists now take the view that successful retirement is all about making sure that you acquire new social roles to replace the ones that you have lost by leaving work, and activities of this sort are exactly the way that people do that.

AGEING

It used to be thought that ageing was a steady decline in functioning, with people going inevitably downhill from the age of 50 or so. But now we know that this is not so.

The general pattern seems to be that we have only a very gradual decline in our older years, and that decline can be slowed down by exercise and activity. Eventually, though, we reach a period of more rapid physical decline, which rarely lasts for more than about five years.

How inevitable the decline is, once it has begun, is something nobody knows. We do know, though, that even old bodies can respond surprisingly well to exercise. In one study, 90-year-olds who began a programme of physical exercises were found to be putting on muscle mass as a result – in other words, their muscles were responding to the exercise and becoming stronger. This finding has been repeated a number of times now, and it shows that the saying 'it's never too late' may be even truer than we realize.

The real danger in ageing, more than any other, seems to be the person's own beliefs about it. Someone who expects to decline and become incapable as they grow older is not likely to face their body or mind with extra challenges. Without exercise, our bodies have no incentive to grow stronger or to maintain their normal levels of strength; so they become weaker. This, to the person who expects to be weak as a result of age, is 'proof' that they were right, and their belief in inevitable decline is confirmed. But really, it began as a self-fulfilling prophecy.

INTELLIGENCE AND AGEING

Intelligence is often inaccurately cited as one of the areas which declines with age. For many years, people 'knew' that various abilities, including intelligence and physical strength, reached their peak in the early twenties, and then declined steadily from then on throughout a person's life.

The problem was that all of these studies were done using cross-sectional methods. That is, the researcher tested several different groups of people, of different ages. But someone who was 60 in 1930 had experienced quite a different upbringing and lifestyle from someone who was 20 at that time.

It wasn't surprising, for example, that older people did badly on intelligence tests in the 1960s, when they had experienced an education which consisted, in the main, of learning large chunks of information off by heart. Younger people, by contrast, had experienced a form of education which stressed reasoning and mental skills, and so they naturally performed much better in IQ tests.

When psychologists actually began to look at how individual people developed, following them up through their lives, a very different picture emerged. For example, in 1966, Burns reported on a study of intelligence and ageing which had begun in the 1920s with a group of teachers who were just emerging from their training colleges. The researchers tested the teachers' intelligence throughout their careers and found that, contrary to what the cross-sectional research showed, their IQ scores had actually increased as they had become older. The apparently inevitable decline with ageing wasn't inevitable at all!

What was even more interesting was the particular scores which the teachers had obtained in their IQ tests. The tests assessed intelligence in two parts: verbal intelligence, which was to do with the use of words and knowledge of vocabulary, and numerical intelligence, which included the use of symbols and logical reasoning as well as arithmetical abilities. When the researchers looked at these scores, they found that the 'arts' teachers, who taught subjects such as English and history, showed an increase in their verbal intelligence scores, but a slight (though not very great) decline in numerical intelligence. The science teachers, though, showed an increase in their numerical intelligence but a slight decline in their verbal intelligence scores.

What this clearly implied was that, more than anything else, it is the amount of practice we have which determines whether or not we are likely to improve our intelligence as we get older. If we adopt a passive mental approach to living, just receiving information passively and not bothering to learn new things unless we absolutely have to, it's likely that our intelligence would decline. Our muscles waste away if we don't use them and, in the same way, our intelligence declines if we don't use it. But if we remain active in our thinking, and ready to learn new things or to challenge our previous assumptions, then we are likely to retain our intelligence, and even increase it. The more we use a skill, the better we get at it.

MEMORY AND AGEING

Most people believe that memory inevitably declines as we get older. However, when a group of people aged between 20 and 36 were compared with a group of people aged between 69 and 80, researchers found that the younger people actually experienced more memory failures than the older people!

It was possible, of course, that the younger people forgot more simply because they had more going on in their lives. But when the researchers repeated the study, this time with a group of people who were still working, aged between 50 and 60, they found an even stronger difference between the two groups. Again, the younger people were much more forgetful than those who were older, even with information that they were trying to remember.

So why are older people so convinced that their memories are poorer now than they were when they were young?

Young people, by and large, don't worry too much about their mental abilities. Older people, though, sensitized by society's belief in an inevitable decline in mental ability with ageing, do worry about it. So when a younger person forgets their key, or can't remember someone's name, or forgets what they came into the room to do, they hardly notice it because it simply doesn't matter to them. When an older person does the same thing, though, it sticks in the mind because they are always wondering if it is a sign of age.

A psychological decline with ageing, then, isn't nearly as inevitable as it once appeared to be. If we use our mental abilities, we are more likely to improve them than to lose them, at least until the very final years of our life. For people who lead full and active lives, and don't hesitate to make efforts or to stretch themselves a little, it seems that they can retain their abilities almost to the end of their lives, with only a relatively sudden decline in the last five years, rather than a continuous steady one.

Sugarman (1986) identified four central ideas in lifespan developmental psychology. The first of these is the idea that development always needs to be seen in its **social context**. How people develop is influenced by their society, their family, their social class and their culture, and social influence can come from many other sources as well. So we can't really study development without taking these into account.

The second idea which Sugarman identified is to do with the fact that social influence isn't just a one-way process. People influence one another, and are influenced by others – it's a two-way process, which we call **reciprocal influence**. This influence isn't static either – it changes all the time. We are influenced by family members and by changes happening within the family, as well as by changes among our friends and work colleagues. And we exert our own influence on these changes as they develop.

Reciprocal influence is important, but it's far from being the whole story. We are also active **agents** in our own lives, making our own choices and decisions. In that sense, we are all active in shaping our own development, and how we understand what is going on is an important aspect of that. For example, as we saw earlier, we know that mental abilities don't inevitably decline with age, but someone who believed firmly that they did decline would tend to 'take it easy' and avoid challenging situations as they grew older, because they wouldn't think it was worth trying. And because of this, they would decline faster than someone who understood lifespan development in a more positive way.

Another fundamental principle that Sugarman identified in lifespan psychology is that of **complexity**. Essentially, this is the same principle that we have encountered so often throughout this book. People are not simple beings, and no single approach is going to be enough to tell us about human beings. We have to take into account different levels of explanation, and to explore connections and issues which arise from them, if we are to get any useful awareness of what human beings are really like.

SUMMARY

Children show the beginnings of social understanding even as toddlers, in that they learn to tease parents and siblings, and will try to comfort those who are upset. They usually achieve the basics of social understanding between three and four years old, and continue to develop it as they go through childhood. It used to be thought that adolescence was always stormy, but we now know that most people pass through adolescence reasonably smoothly. Resolving the role confusion of adolescence is just one of eight psychosocial conflicts which we may need to resolve throughout our lifespans.

Early studies of ageing implied that decline was inevitable, but modern studies have shown that this is the case only at the very end of our lives. Effectively, it is a question of 'use it or lose it', a dictum that applies to mental abilities as well as to physical ones. We can improve our mental skills with practice even late in life. Lifespan psychology emphasizes complexity and social context, and sees people as active agents in their lives, exerting reciprocal influences on the others around them.

SUNDAY
MONDAY
TUESDAY
WEDNESDAY
THURSDAY
FRIDAY
SATURDAY

FACT-CHECK (ANSWERS AT THE BACK)

1. Which of the following are important examples of interaction during childhood?
   a) Teasing ❑
   b) Encouragement ❑
   c) Comforting ❑
   d) All of the above ❑

2. At what age, roughly, does a child become fully aware of the existence of others as independent individuals?
   a) Two ❑
   b) Seven ❑
   c) Three and a half ❑
   d) Five ❑

3. Vygotsky's idea of how much others can support a child's development is the:
   a) Zone of normal development ❑
   b) Zone of proximal development ❑
   c) Pre-operational stage ❑
   d) Zone of arctic development ❑

4. What is the first stage of childhood cognitive development, according to Piaget?
   a) The pre-operational stage ❑
   b) The concrete operational stage ❑
   c) The sensory/motor stage ❑
   d) None of the above ❑

5. Bandura argued that:
   a) A turbulent adolescence was normal ❑
   b) All adolescents are inevitably disturbed ❑
   c) Many adolescents improve their relationships with parents ❑
   d) Fashion is the most important thing for Western adolescents ❑

6. What, according to Erikson, was the classic conflict of adolescence?
   a) Autonomy vs shame ❑
   b) Industry vs inferiority ❑
   c) Identity vs role confusion ❑
   d) Intimacy vs isolation ❑

7. ...And what was Erikson's classic conflict of maturity?
   a) Industry vs inferiority ❑
   b) Intimacy vs isolation ❑
   c) Integrity vs despair ❑
   d) Generativity vs stagnation ❑

8. Which of the following are typically major transitions in late maturity?
   a) Marriage ❑
   b) Retirement ❑
   c) Mid-life crisis ❑
   d) Parenthood ❑

9. Intelligence...
   a) Declines with age ❑
   b) Remains static throughout life ❑
   c) Improves with practice ❑
   d) None of the above ❑

10. Why do older people worry about their memory?

a) Because the memory function declines after the age of about 50 ❏

b) Because the societal myth of memory loss in later life has sensitized them ❏

c) Because memories matter more to them ❏

d) None of the above ❏

SUNDAY

MONDAY

TUESDAY

WEDNESDAY

THURSDAY

FRIDAY

SATURDAY

APPENDIX: WHAT DO PSYCHOLOGISTS DO?

Psychologists always specialize in one way or another. Academic psychologists, for example, generally work within a very small area of psychology. Their task is to conduct research into that area, identifying the fundamental mechanisms and processes which are taking place, and exploring how they can contribute to our understanding of people.

Professional psychologists also tend to specialize, dealing with just one area of applied psychology. They use the work of academic psychologists and also conduct research of their own, and put that knowledge to use in helping people in one way or another. Their research also feeds back into academic psychology – in fact, most areas of academic psychology have been influenced at one time or another by theories and evidence obtained from professional or applied psychology.

THE PSYCHOLOGICAL PROFESSIONS

Professional psychologists can be found at work in almost any area which involves dealing with people. Forensic psychologists, for example, work with police and prison staff in tackling many different aspects of crime. Sports psychologists work with coaches and competitors, developing ways of maximizing competitive performance. Consumer psychologists are at work in advertising and market research, working out how to reach new markets.

Professional training for psychologists takes many years – typically, three years for a first degree, followed by another three years in specialist work and a couple more years in supervised practice. But there are other types of work that psychologists do too. As a rule, people who begin to study psychology don't usually know what area of work they want to go into when they have finished. What they do know is that they are interested in people and want to learn more about them.

DEVELOPING PSYCHOLOGICAL KNOWLEDGE

How do psychologists gain their knowledge? People, as we have seen, are extremely complex, and understanding the ways that our minds work is never going to be a matter of one simple explanation. Everything we do is influenced by a diverse range of experiences, from our biochemical state to the culture we were brought up in and the situation we are in right now. It's the psychologist's task to bring all these together and try to make sense of them.

Psychologists, though, are scientists, and most psychological knowledge is developed as a result of some kind of empirical research. As researchers, psychologists tend to work only in one small area at a time. It isn't possible to conduct research into the whole of human nature – we have to concentrate on just one bit at a time, or everything would be too complicated. So quite a lot of psychological knowledge consists of small bits of research, each of which can throw a little light onto a situation, but they aren't enough to explain it on their own.

This means that it is very important for psychology to have ways of linking together those pieces of research, so that they can form coherent explanations for what is going on. Scientific explanations are known as **theories**, and they are just as important in psychological knowledge as empirical research. Without theories to bring together research findings and make sense of them, there wouldn't be much point in doing research in the first place, because it wouldn't really tell us anything – it would just be a collection of 'ooh-look-ain't-it-interesting' facts, and we can get those from quiz shows or everyday observation.

Actually, just about all psychological research is driven by theory in the first place. People conduct research in order to investigate whether a particular theory is true; and their findings are obtained in such a way that they can test the theory, to see how well it holds up in reality. It's all very well having a plausible idea, but lots of plausible ideas really don't work very well when we actually look closely at human beings. Part of the definition of a scientific theory is that it can be tested against empirical evidence, and challenged or refuted if it doesn't seem to work. There are other kinds of theories which don't exactly work in the same way, but we don't usually count these as scientific ones.

Even theories, though, can generally deal with only one aspect of human functioning at once. If we really want to get to grips with what human beings do, we need to look at it using several different levels of analysis at the same time. **Levels of analysis**, which are sometimes known as levels of explanation, are all about the way that we choose to study something.

If we wanted to look into the human activity known as reading, for example, we might decide to study it by investigating what happens to the nerve cells in the brain as we read. This would be the **neurological** level of analysis, because we would be studying the neurones which are involved in that activity. Another psychologist, though, might choose to look at reading in terms of how we process the information that we receive, mentally. This would be the **cognitive** level of analysis, because it is concerned with our cognitions – how we perceive, remember and apply information that we come across in everyday life. A third psychologist might choose to study reading in terms of its functions in society – what children and adults learn from books and other publications, and how this influences social living. This would be the **socio-cultural** level of analysis.

All these levels of analysis, and quite a few others, are involved in understanding reading. Although we might conduct research into only one level at a time, getting the whole picture of what is going on when people read needs all of them. So if they are really about explaining human behaviour, the theories that we develop need to be able to bring together, or at least connect with, several different levels of explanation.

Most psychological research is about gathering evidence. That evidence might be used to support or refute the theories which have been developed to explain what is going on; or it might be used to identify how interventions may be more effective. Gathering psychological evidence is a bit like detective work. It is always easy to jump to conclusions about an answer. If a crime has been committed, you can always find someone who is certain who is responsible – but sometimes they are completely wrong. In the same way, when we are studying something in psychology, it is easy to jump to conclusions about it. After all, we all think we know about human beings. But sometimes, as with the crime, our conclusions are simply wrong.

So the psychologist, like the detective, has to put in hours of painstaking work collecting evidence, to find out what is really going on. Sometimes all that evidence will lead to the same conclusion we might have obtained by guessing, or from 'common sense'. But even though our conclusions might not be earth-shattering, at least we know that they are based on a solid foundation. Quite often, though, what we discover is totally unpredictable. And without collecting the evidence in the first place, we would never have known it.

GLOSSARY

accommodation The process by which a schema is stretched or changed to take account of new information or fresh learning

anticipatory schemas The mental structures we develop to help us make sense of the world and of the situations we are likely to encounter

assimilation The way that an existing **schema** absorbs new information without having to change

association learning *See* **conditioning**.

attribution In psychology, term used to describe the process by which people give reasons for why something has happened or why others behave the way they do

circadian rhythm The daily cycle of physiological changes and associated emotional states experienced by humans and other animals

co-evolution The mutual evolution of animals and their environment

cognition Mental processes; the related adjective is **cognitive**.

cognitive therapy A therapeutic practice that aims to help people address their problems by changing and/or managing the way they think about themselves, other people and situations

conditioning A form of learning in which a particular stimulus produces a particular response; in its most fundamental form known as **classical conditioning**

defence mechanism A mental process by which the human mind protects itself against harmful events or situations

discourse analysis Scientific examination of the way people express themselves in language – the words they choose, how they say them and the social meanings contained within the discourse itself

fight-or-flight response Survival instinct in all animals that causes the body to go into overdrive, providing the energy either to fight or flee a predator; in humans, often related to feelings of stress.

lateral thinking An ability to think in fresh or unexpected ways

limerance A state of mind characterized by passionate, uncontrollable romantic feelings for another, as defined by Dorothy Tennov

mental set A fixed or closed way of thinking, determined by our expectations. *Compare* **lateral thinking**.

one-trial learning Behaviour learned when an individual makes a strong connection between a stimulus and a response after only one exposure.

perceptual set A way of perceiving the physical world around us that is determined by our expectations

psychology The scientific study of experience and behaviour

psychoanalysis The therapeutic practice most closely associated with the ideas of Sigmund Freud and his followers

schema *See* **anticipatory schema**.

self-actualization The development, or actualization, of the potential of the self or personality

self-concept Each individual's ideas about himself or herself

social representations Beliefs, values and ideas shared by a society, group or community

social script An accepted pattern of behaviour widely understood by members of a society, group or community as the appropriate thing to do in that situation

stress Long-term emotional arousal in response to fear or anxiety that can have harmful effects, both psychologically and physiologically

theory of mind The awareness of others as independent thinking individuals

transition In developmental psychology, a term applied to a crucial passage from one life stage to another, e.g. from adolescence to adulthood

unconditional positive regard Regard given to an individual no matter how he or she acts; an important basis for healthy psychological development

zone of proximal development According to Lev Vygotsky, the part of a child's potential that can be developed through guidance and structure provided by other people (e.g. teachers or carers).

REFERENCES

Asch, S.E. (1952). *Social Psychology*. Englewood Cliffs, NJ: Prentice Hall.

Bandura, A. (1997). *Self-efficacy: The Exercise of Control*. New York: W.H. Freeman.

Bartlet, F. (1932). *Remembering*. Cambridge University Press, Cambridge, 1932.

Gardner, H. (1983). *Frames of Mind: The Theory of Multiple Intelligences* (1983).

Gibson, J.J. (1982). *Reasons for Realism: Selected Essays of James J. Gibson*, ed. E. Reed and R. Jones. Hillsdale, NJ: Lawrence Erlbaum.

Gould, E. (1978). *Transformations: Growth and Change in Adult Life*. New York: Simon & Schuster.

Harré, H.R. (1979). *Social Being: A Theory for a Social Psychology II*. Oxford: Blackwell, 1979.

Loftus, E.F., and Palmer, J.C. (1974). 'Reconstruction of automobile destruction: an example of the interaction between language and memory'. *Journal of Verbal Learning and Verbal Behavior* 13: 585–9.

Morris, P.E., Gruneberg, M.M., Sykes, R.N., and Merrick, A. (1981). 'Football knowledge and the acquisition of new results', *British Journal of Psychology* 72: 479–83.

Moscovici, S., and Nemeth, C. (1974). *Social Psychology: Classic and Contemporary Integrations* (7th edn). Oxford: Rand Mcnally.

Seligman, M.E.P. (2002). *Authentic Happiness: Using the New Positive Psychology to Realize Your Potential for Lasting Fulfillment*. New York: Free Press.

Seyle, H. (1956). *The Stress of Life*. New York: McGraw-Hill, 1956.

Sternberg, Robert J., and Barnes, Michael L. (1988), *The Psychology of Love*. Yale University Press

Sugarman, L. (1986). *Life-span Development: Concepts, Theories and Interventions*. London: Methuen.

Tennov, D. (1979). *Love and Limerence*. Lanham, MD: Scarborough House.

Wagner, W., and Hayes, N. (2005). *Everyday Discourse and Common-sense: The Theory of Social Representation*. New York: Palgrave Macmillan.

ANSWERS

Sunday: 1c; 2a; 3b & c; 4d; 5c; 6a; 7d; 8b; 9c; 10b

Monday: 1c; 2c; 3a; 4c; 5c; 6b; 7b; 8d; 9b; 10c

Tuesday: 1d; 2c; 3c; 4d; 5a; 6c; 7d; 8a; 9d; 10a

Wednesday: 1c; 2b; 3d; 4d; 5c; 6b; 7b; 8d; 9b; 10a & b

Thursday: 1b; 2d; 3a; 4c; 5c; 6b; 7a; 8c; 9c; 10b

Friday: 1a; 2b; 3c; 4b; 5a; 6d; 7b; 8d; 9b; 10c

Saturday: 1d; 2c; 3b; 4c; 5c; 6c; 7d; 8b; 9c; 10b